AF882250

generation/mutation

Published by Topos Media Books
An imprint of Topos Productions
1050 Queen Street, Suite 100
Honolulu, HI 96814
USA

toposmediabooks.com

Copyright © 2020 Topos Productions

All rights reserved. Except for the quotation of short passages for the purposes of criticism and review, no part of this publication may be reproduced, stored in a retrieval system, or transmitted, in any form or by any means, electronic, mechanical, photocopying, recording or otherwise, without the prior permission of the publisher.

ISBN 978-1-94335-403-0

generation/mutation

from crowdsourced to ai-sourced
new media art

Holger 'H-Ray' Heine

For Suzanne

Contents

Preface

This book tells the story of *generation/mutation,* a collaborative new media art project that—after more than two decades of online life—continues to evolve in new and unexpected directions.

The original project, *generation/mutation* 1.0, was launched in 1998. It succeeded in crowdsourcing all creative work online—years before the expression "crowdsourcing" was even coined! An international group of forty-five artists contributed works to version 1.0 of the project. The resulting online exhibition was seen by more than 2,5 million visitors during its first three years online! Then, in 2006, an un-expected "renaissance" of the project became possible with the introduction of Google Street View and Google Earth services which led to the addition of machine-sourced contributions. Finally, beginning in 2018, one more mutation of the project generated a third collection of contributions—a collection of ai-sourced works, generated by artificial intelligence (AI) applications and machine learning algorithms.

In the two decades since the project was launched, *generation/mutation* evolved from an online exhibition showing crowd-sourced contributions created by human artists to the inclusion of machine-made contributions found on Google Street View to completely ai-generated contributions using neural style transfer (NST) technologies.

The original idea for *generation/mutation* was quite simple: visitors to the project website were invited to download a "seed" image, change that image in any way they want, and then send the result back for inclusion in the project's online exhibition.

The response to the original version of *generation/mutation* was simply amazing. In the first two years, over two million visitors came to explore the online presentation of the crowdsourced contributions! A jaw-dropping number for a small, independent new media project at a time when a turnout of just a hundred visitors to a brick and mortar gallery opening would have been considered a resounding success!

Over time, *generation/mutation* took on a life of its own and became (a very small) part of popular online culture—the project enjoyed its fifteen seconds of Internet fame. If it wasn't for that peculiar persistence of digital memory—one of the unintended side effects of modern Internet search engines—*generation/mutation v.1.0* might have ended as a footnote in the history of new media art.

But the evolution of web-based technologies created the foundations for a second and third mutation of the project. The second mutation of the project, *generation/mutation* 2.0, presents a collection of machine-made contributions—images found on Google's Street View and Google Earth services. The Google-made images were taken at same location that is seen in the original seed image and present a Street View interpretation of the same place.

Finally, the third mutation of the project presents images that are made by AI—generated by the application of neural style transfer models that became accessible as early as 2018. The images presented in the third mutation return to the original seed image but they now render the original image based on the visual "style" detected in a second image, for example, an image of a painting by Vincent Van Gogh or Auguste Renoir or Mark Rothko.

There is an interesting shift in meaning that the full names of blue chip artists take on in the age of AI-generated art. A person's full name refers to the individual, the human being, and the work created by him or her. The artworld already has transformed artist's last names into trademarks, brands, and genres. It is easy to see how this trajectory will find new extensions through the application of AI and machine learning technologies. "Paint a Van Gogh landscape of London Tower Bridge" is as valid and realizable an instruction to an application of neural style transfer algorithms as is "Write a short novel Pynchon-style about a fifty-two-year-old beatnik writer living in San Francisco in the 1970's" to one of the recent text generators like GPT-3.

The neural style transfer images in *generation/mutation 3.0* illustrate the imitative power of machine learning applications. But they also show their limitations, especially their lack of genuine creativity. The algorithms produce high level simulations of activities we used to think of as uniquely human. Now we have reached a point where we need to come to terms with simulations of creative behavior that are increasingly difficult to distinguish from genuine expressions of human creativity.

The sheer longevity of *generation/mutation*, spanning more than twenty years, sets it apart from most works within the rapidly moving domain of new media art. It also creates a unique opportunity to reflect on the cultural and social changes brought about by the explosive growth of the Internet during the lifetime of the project. It was the creation of global, digital networks that made *generation/mutation* possible in the first place. The continuing technical revolutions that took place during the last two decades shaped and re-shaped the creative composition of *generation/ mutation* at three decisive points in its evolution: First the emergence of new creative practices and art-making techniques based on global digital networks; then the introduction of machine-generated photographic mapping systems; and, finally, the emergence of AI-driven creative methods and the new breed of artworks engendered by this somewhat opaque technology.

Just as the invention of photography freed painting from its bondage to the visible, the rise of AI and creative machines frees today's artists from their bondage to traditional art-making practices. We can only wait and see where this newly found freedom will take a new generation of artists. In its two decades of development, *generation/mutation* has become both chronicle and manifestation of this transition and liberation.

All three versions of *generation/mutation* are presented together for the first time in this volume. The original version, *generation/mutation* 1.0, has been available only as an online presentation. It is presented here in print for the first time. Versions 2.0 and 3.0 of the project have not been shown before at all. It is only with the publication of this volume that they are made available to a broad audience.

Many have helped this project come to realization. Suzanne Savet, Malcolm Rose-Heine, Wilma Heine, Christine Amoros, Jeremy Turner, Heike Baars, Fung Lin Hall, Sabine Hannen, Tina Foster, Chris and Vicky Ingalls, Detlev Voormann, Gloria and Armando Savet, Carolyn Koo, and Todd Manley, all supported the project from the moment they first learned about it. Elisabeth Presa and David Shea at the University of Melbourne VCA Centre for Ideas allowed me to further develop the project while teaching at the Centre.

Joyce Saku Charlton, Udo Hanten, Lee Nasso, and my father Wolfgang Heine saw the beginnings of *generation/ mutation,* but left this world before the project had reached its conclusion. I will always remember them with love and gratitude.

Finally, and most importantly, a special "Thank You!" to the artists of the first—crowdsourced—version of *generation/ mutation*. It was their creativity and skill and trust and support that made it possible for *generation/mutation* to become such an enduring success.

Holger 'H-Ray' Heine

December 2020, Honolulu, Hawaii

generation/mutation

As for the whole, it is preserved by the perpetual mutation and conversion of simple elements one into another and by the mutation and alteration of things mixed and compounded.

Marcus Aurelius, *Meditations*

1.0 Crowds

The original version of *generation/mutation* was launched on DIGITALSOULS.COM in March of 1998 with a simple call to artists.[1] The call consisted of a few hand-coded HTML pages: a project description, a downloadable 41 Kb JPEG image file, and three instructions. Participating artists were asked to

- download the project's seed image
- alter the image any way they like
- email the result back to be shown in an online exhibition.

Participation in the project was open to everyone and every contribution—provided it met a few simple technical requirements—was guaranteed a place in the planned online exhibition. No jury, no curator, no censorship. The aim was to trigger a free and open-ended collaboration that would generate a series of contributions by artists from around the world, using the just emerging Internet as the only means of communication and exchange.

From today's point of view, a simple and familiar concept. In 1998, however, the project was an early exploration of the opportunities afforded by this amazing new thing called the Internet. At the time, the Internet was nothing like the common place feature of everyday life that it is today. Even in technophile San Francisco, the Internet was still a rather obscure technological innovation, largely unnoticed in popular culture. To try to harness the possibilities of digital connectivity to generate a new kind of collaborative online artwork was a revolutionary and untested undertaking. And—just like the outcome of revolutions in general—the outcome of *generation/mutation* was more than uncertain!

The question was: Is the World Wide Web ready to sustain a project like *generation/mutation*? Is it a viable foundation for the project? Are there enough artists online to make it work? And even if there are enough online denizens ready to participate in the project, how would they find out about *generation/mutation* in the first place?[2]

The biggest unknown at the start of the project was the intended method of receiving contributions. *Crowdsourcing* as a method of outsourcing services or work to a crowd of online contributors did not yet exist. Even the concept of crowdsourcing itself was not easy to grasp, even for the more visionary Internet users of the day. To try to outsource *creative work* over the Internet in order to curate an online exhibition of crowd-sourced artworks was truly a bit "out there" – to put it mildly. But that is exactly what *generation/mutation* set out to do. Not only did *generation/mutation* employ crowdsourcing as its only method to acquire contributions for an online exhibition, it did so *avant la lettre*, some seven years before the word "crowdsourcing" was coined in San Francisco in 2005![3]

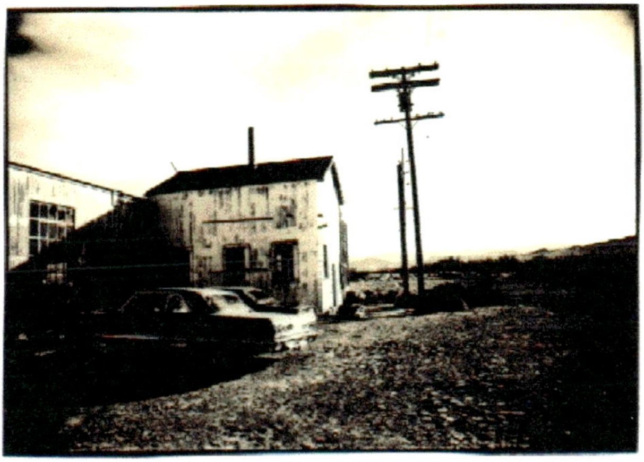

Death Valley Junction 1981
Isochromatic transparency generated from a 35mm b/w negative
Filename: dv01.jpg

Seed image for *generation/mutation*. Distributed as downloadable file for manipulation by contributors

Original photograph: Holger 'H-Ray' Heine (1981)
Kodak b/w film. Nikon F2A, 24mm

By comparison, the other core method employed by *generation/mutation*, the practice of using a set of instructions to direct the creation of a work of art from a distance had been frequently used in contemporary art since the beginning of the twentieth century. It was Marcel Duchamp, who pioneered the practice in 1916 when he wrote from New York to his sister Suzanne in Paris, asking her to add the inscription "*d'après Marcel Duchamp*" ("after Marcel Duchamp") to an ordinary bottle rack that he had kept in his studio. At the time, Duchamp considered the bottle rack a piece of sculpture that was "already made" and he had kept it unaltered in his studio. After discovering the American expression "readymade" soon after his arrival in New York, Duchamp's intention was not only to create his first readymade work, but to do this remotely, via instructions in a letter.

However, as fate would have it, Duchamp's sister had already thrown away the bottle rack—an ordinary house-hold item of the times—while cleaning out her brother's Paris studio a few days before his letter reached her. Con-sequently, the first of Duchamp's readymades started out as a strictly conceptual work without a material instantiation.[4] Not only that, *Bottle Rack* was also the first "pure" readymade in that it did not involve any alteration of the object by the artist at all.[5]

More recently, the use of instructions for the production and curation of artworks is often associated with the work of Hans Ulrich Obrist and, especially, his *Do It* project (Independent Curators International 2020). Obrist developed Duchamp's concept of creating artworks via instructions into a curatorial practice that produced a unique collection of artist instructions including performance pieces, urban interventions, philosophical reflections—even recipes—from artists like Louise Bourgeois, Douglas Coupland, Sol LeWitt, David Lynch, Lawrence Weiner, and Ai Weiwei.

Maria Popova (2013), in her apt description of the project, notes that *Do it*

> explores art as unbridling of author and authority, art as internationalism, art as a homage and a middle finger to Art. It lives somewhere between Yoko Ono's instructions for art and life, John Cage's interpretable notations, and Philip Glass's notion of authorship as transformation (Popova 2013).

The project replaces (or amends) traditional practice of art-making with the enactment or performance of one of the many sets of instructions. As Obrist points out, the project

> rejects the notion of the original in favour of an open-ended conception of the creation of the work and . . . is less concerned with copies, images, or reproductions of artworks, than with human interpretations (Obrist, Do It: The Compendium 2013).

A very important aspect that has contributed to the continued creative potency of the ongoing project is that "no two interpretations of the same set of instructions are ever identical" (Obrist, Ways of Curating 2014).[6]

The same principle underlies the first version of *generation/mutation,* which evolved independently of Obrist's *Do it*. The key feature of *generation/mutation* was the collaborative generation of creative work by crowd-sourced contributors—it was to be an organic, evolving, process-oriented, open access work. The collaboration would rely entirely on the new methods of communication and exchange that were just beginning to be possible through the rapid growth of digital networks and the increasing availability of software and hardware. The ultimate outcome was open, without any pre-determined end, deadline, or final presentation. In this way, *generation/mutation* not only realized the idea of art as an open-ended and ongoing process—it also succeeded in functioning as a generative work. Brian Eno described this perspective on art and art-making when he pointed out that since the beginning of the twentieth century,

> artists have been moving away from an idea of art as something finished, perfect, definitive and unchanging towards a view of artworks as processes or the seeds for processes – things that exist and change in time, things that are never finished (Eno 2001).

For *generation/mutation,* this meant that if artists sent contributions, their work would be added to the online gallery and the project would continue to grow.[7] In addition, the new contributions themselves are open to appropriation and alteration by participating artists, just like the original seed image.

The small number of rules created new possibilities for branches of development that, over time, could generate a tree-like structure of contributions.[8] It was an approach that set out to implement Eno's concept of generative and process-oriented artmaking in which

> artworks in general are increasingly regarded as seeds – seeds for processes that need a viewer's (or a whole culture's) active mind in which to develop. Increasingly working with time, culture-makers see themselves as people who start things, not finish them (Eno 2001)

For *generation/mutation,* as an online project, any hope for success in translating this concept of artworks as seeds into a broad, online collaboration depended on the state of the World Wide Web and its denizens.

When *generation/mutation* was launched in 1998, the World Wide Web was not yet ten years old. To most people—if they even had heard of it in the first place—the Web was something futuristic, an unfamiliar and unexplored territory. To many, it did not have any clear use or purpose. It was a trendy and hip playground for techno-geeks and increasingly popular with researchers and scientists in universities or multinational corporations, but in general, the World Wide Web was still a rather obscure technology that played no part in most people's lives.

Invented by Tim Berners-Lee in 1989 as an information sharing system, the World Wide Web introduced the now familiar communication tools and infrastructure of digital networks: web browsers (TimBL coded the first one in 1990, released to the public in 1991), servers and routers, essential languages like HTML (Hyper Text Markup Language), connection protocols like http and ftp, URL's and IP addresses, domain names, websites, email, multi-media content consisting of images, video, audio, and text—all of it had to be invented or transformed into the building blocks of TimBL's World Wide Web.

Nine years later, in 1998 in the San Francisco Bay Area—the technophile cultural home and creative background for *generation/mutation*—the World Wide Web, websites, even email, were still new and unfamiliar things to most people. Much of what was to become basic and ubiquitous features of today's online world was associated with computer geeks and weirdos, people who tinkered in basements and garages with electronic circuit boards, soldering irons, high-speed 9600 baud dialup modems, and assortments of green or orange monochrome monitors.

At the same time, there was a growing awareness of the Internet and WWW among creatives, artists of all genres, especially musicians, image makers (film, video, graphic design), basically anyone who was interested in the intersection of art and technology. Many of them purchased their first personal computers and a dial-up modem and became early explorers of digital and network technologies.

Getting online, however, required considerable technical skill. Modems had to be configured, web browsers and email clients had to be downloaded and installed, and all that just to stumble upon webpages that took forever to download and which, after the long wait, did not even provide the information that one had been looking for . . .

Nevertheless, the total number of Internet users was growing at an astonishing speed. And so was the number of websites. Early in 1998, the World Wide Web included 1 million registered domain names. But only a fraction of the names had a website attached to them. And even if they did, many "websites" at the time consisted of only a single, hard-coded HTML webpage with some text and a few pictures. Worldwide, about 120 million users accessed the Web, creating a ratio of approximately 108 users per available website (Internet Live Stats 2019). First generation popular search engines like Altavista, AOL, Infoseek, Lycos, Hotbot, or Yahoo helped users navigate the rapidly growing web (Wikipedia 2018).

It was the time before Google, Facebook, or Amazon—the dawn of the World Wide Web. The algorithms for a revolutionary new search engine were still a mere vision in the minds of Sergey Brin and Larry Page. At the time, both were working on their first search engine named *BackRub* at Stanford University (Brin 2016). The domain name google.com was first registered on September 15, 1997, but the public search engine did not go online until 1998, the same year *generation/mutation* was launched (Google 2016).

At the time, the dramatic and frequent shortcomings of existing search engines led to a growing popularity of human edited directories. Human edited directories provided reliably much better results compared to the popular software based search engines. One of these human edited directories proved crucial for *generation/mutation* in finding its audience and contributors: DMOZ.ORG, a human edited website index, part of the Open Directory Project. The dmoz.org listings for digitalsouls.com and *generation/mutation* helped bring a significant number of new visitors to the site.

In addition to the listings on DMOZ.ORG and Yahoo.com, the launch of Netscape's Communicator software package in June of 1997 was another important factor that directly contributed to the early success of *generation/mutation*. While Netscape's Navigator browser already had re-defined how a web browser should look and function and, in the process, it had changed the perception and experience of the World Wide Web for millions of users. Text and images, even videos and audio clips could now be viewed together on a single webpage. The Netscape's Communicator suite featured its flagship Navigator browser and included an email client, an address book (contact manager), a newsgroup reader and even a WYSIWIG (*What You See Is What You Get*) HTML editor (Wikipedia 2016).[9] The strong popularity of the Navigator browser was clearly visible in the visitor stats for *generation/mutation* where more than 60% percent used a Netscape browser during the first three years online.

Of course, learning about *generation/mutation* in some form or other and to be able to access the project's website was just the first step. To participate in the project, artists not only had to access the Internet with one of the early web browsers, they also needed to find the call to artists and download the seed image from the website to their own computer. In addition, artists then needed access to some type of image processing software.

Adobe Photoshop, CorelDRAW, Paint Shop and many other programs were readily available, but Photoshop established itself from the beginning as industry leader. In May 1998, two months after the call for artists for *generation/mutation* had been posted, Photoshop 5.0—codenamed 'Strange Cargo'—was released.[10]

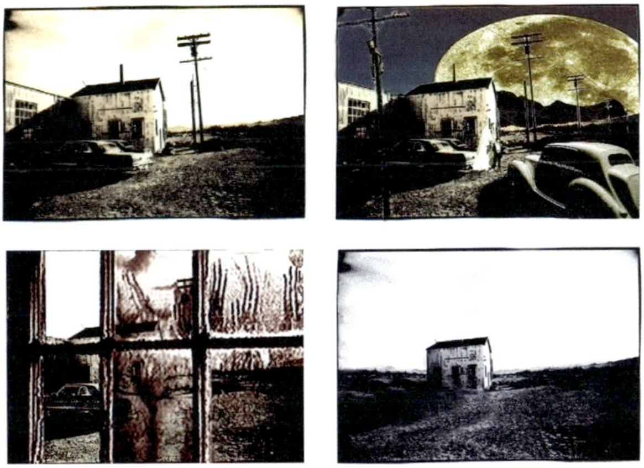

Selection 1 (clockwise from top left) – H-Ray Heine: Death Valley Junction 1982 (seed image), Carl Patzel: Moon Valley, Phil Smith: untitled, Mary Lynch: untitled

This version featured innovations like a repeating "undo" command, new color management settings, and—perhaps the greatest new addition—the "magnetic" lasso, a selection tool that automatically clings to prominent outlines in an image, making it easier to pick out shapes and figures in a layer for copying or other manipulations (Wikipedia 2019). The technological innovations included in 'Strange Cargo' illustrate the overall state of the art for image manipulation software at the time.

The broader impact of image manipulation software was a severe disruption of the traditional trust in the truthfulness of the photographic image and its depiction of objects and events in the world. This new level of uncertainty and caution about the fidelity of photographic images grew from the realization of how easy it had become to create convincingly "real" looking photographic images that are nevertheless completely fake. Of course, it had been possible to "doctor" photographs before the appearance of digital image manipulation software, but the mostly manual processes had been much more difficult and required skilled professionals and their expertise. With the growing ubiquity (and the new normal) of image manipulations of all sorts, from enhancements to sophisticated fakes, *photoshop* became a verb. Photographic images no longer guarantee a fundamental truthfulness. The general possibility that any image that we see has been "photoshopped" precludes any naïve assumptions about the truthfulness of the "photographic" image.

In this vertiginous and brave new world of digital image production and consumption, the "photographic" image is *prima facie* suspect because of its "photo-realistic" appearance, revealing the image as something that—at some level—has been constructed and generated for a purpose. Reality as such is no longer needed as the point of origin and source of truth. Like paintings before them, photographic images in the digital realm no longer require a direct link back to anything 'real' at all. Pixels are the ontological bedrock of digital visual presentation but, as bits of digital information, no single source of truth beyond code exists.

To demand a method of verification by which the correspondence between image and objective reality could be determined is to misapprehend the new—digital—nature of the visual presentations of the real.

Fred Ritchin (2013) observed the potential of Photoshop to devalue the photographic image as a "document of social communication" because of the erosion of the traditional value of photographs as evidence. He notes that

> there used to be a time when one could show people a photograph and the image would have the weight of evidence—the "camera never lies." Certainly, photography always lied, but as a mechanical reproduction of visual appearances it was something viewers generally accepted as a truthful representation of whatever it happened to depict (Ritchin 2013).

Today the digital rendering of the visible has become the new norm and the traditional role photography as a technology for the truthful representation of the world has been delegated to the history of the visible. As Ritchin points out, the complete malleability of photographic images and, with it, the complete independence of the photographic image from reality, makes

> photography more of a rhetorical strategy, like words, rather than an automatic proof of anything. Photographs must now persuade, often in concert with other media, rather than rely on a routine perception that they inevitably record the way things are (Ritchin 2013).

The tension between a naïve belief in the mechanical truthfulness of photographic images and the dizzying range of image manipulation techniques plays an important part in the contributions to *generation/mutation*. However, the overall tone of the image manipulations and alterations show more of a playful spirit of exploration and experimentation than the pessimism is found in the more dystopian perspectives on digital technologies.

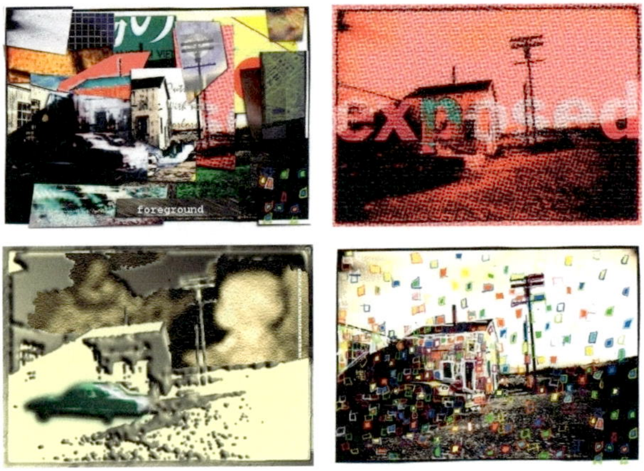

Selection 2 (clockwise from top left) – Kakupacal: untitled, Martin Pribble: *image for alteration,* Kelly Darke: *Squared,* Udo Hanten: *boy Zone*

All the manipulations of the digital seed image include a moment of appropriation of the image file that is similar to the appropriation of the photographed object that Susan Sontag observed in her seminal reflections on the nature of photography.

> To photograph is to appropriate the thing photographed. It means putting oneself into a certain relation to the world that

feels like knowledge—and, therefore, like power (Sontag, On Photography 1977).

All manipulations of the seed image of *generation/mutation* presuppose the appropriation of the image (and the digital file that contains it). But acts of appropriation do not merely *resemble* or "feel like" power—they are *constitutive* of power in the conventional sense. In the case of *generation/mutation*, however, the act of appropriation presents a moment of empowerment and creative independence. Whatever happens next is completely the work of an individual artist.

The first phase of *generation/mutation* was an experiment. The seed image and instructions were like a digital message in a bottle cast into a vast and uncharted digital ocean. The goal of the experiment was to find out if the new connectivity provided by the Internet and the growing availability of digital image processing software could be combined into a new way of making art. This new way of making art would bring together contributions by artists from around the world and present the result in a collectively produced (i.e., crowd-sourced) new media artwork.

Over time, *generation/mutation* evolved into a collaborative meditation on the meaning of images and creative practices in networked world where software is the ontological bedrock upon which virtual universes are built. The project raises crucial questions about digital imagery, artists, creative practices, popular culture, authenticity and visual truth.

As a collective work of art, *generation/mutation* defies traditional assumptions of authorship. It consists of many individual contributions, but it is not the work of a single author or artist. It is a synthesis of voices and expressions that relate to each other and create a presentation that is simultaneously unified and polymorphous. It challenges the traditional roles of artist, artwork, and spectator, and explores the shift from a world that is grounded in a classic account of reality to the new, digital representation of the real, the intersection of the hyper-real and the virtual.

Finally, *generation/mutation* is a deeply philosophical work. Not in the traditional form of a book or academic journal paper, but in the form of a collaborative and creative meditation on the nature of artistic practices at the onset of the twenty-first century, an articulation of a new method of artistic collaboration and exploration.

Notes

[1] DIGITALSOULS.COM just had been launched less than a year before in 1997 as an e-zine and online gallery dedicated to new media art.

[2] This was before Google revolutionized web searches. Search engines still had considerable issues to resolve, to put it mildly. Searching for content was time consuming and often frustrating. Google's public search engine at google.com went online the same year *generation/mutation* was launched.

[3] The expression "crowdsourcing" was coined by Jeff Howe and Mark Robinson, editors at Wired, to describe how companies were beginning to use the Internet to "outsource work to the crowd" (Safire, 2009).

[4] Several versions of *Bottlerack* were created later, beginning with a copy that Duchamp kept in his New York studio in 1915.

[5] In 1919, Duchamp and his sister Suzanne collaborated once more in the creation of second readymade that was realized through the execution of a set of instructions. Back in Paris, Suzanne had married (the just divorced) Jean Crotti, a French painter who she had first met while visiting her brother in New York. Crotti and Duchamp shared a studio on West 67th Street and it was there that Suzanne and Crotti first met. As a wedding gift, Duchamp sent Suzanne his instructions for an "Unhappy readymade" from Buenos Aires. To create the work, Duchamp asked his sister to hang a geometry textbook from the balcony of her Paris apartment and to keep it out in the open, exposed to wind, sun and rain, so that the problems and

theorems could "get the facts of life." Suzanne created the work as described by her brother and painted a picture of the result (Tomkins 1996).

[6] Recently, Google launched an online version of *Do it.* https://artsandculture.google.com/project/do-it

[7] There was something like a "natural" ending of the first phase of *generation/mutation.* Contributions stopped after the 9/11 attacks and the project went dormant until about 2007, when Google Earth and Google Street View opened a second phase for the project: the inclusion of machine-sourced images.

[8] Only a few artists made use of this option. In hindsight, it is possible that the idea was not communicated clearly enough. Either way, a large majority of contributors chose to work with the original seed image, which preserved a greater underlying continuity within the diversity of contributions.

[9] Incidentally, the first versions of *generation/mutation* were hand-coded using Netscape Navigator and its built-in WYSIWIG html editor.

[10] The first version of Photoshop was released in 1990 (Wikipedia 2019).

generation/mutation 1.1
online exhibition

Martin S. Pribble | Jeremy Turner | Donald Trimble | Martin Selman
h-ray heine | Jonathan Prince | Kelly Darke | Zye Zaen | jaxun
Scott Lickstein | Ted Bragg | Elisha Sarti

June 1998

The idea becomes the machine that creates the work.

Sol LeWitt

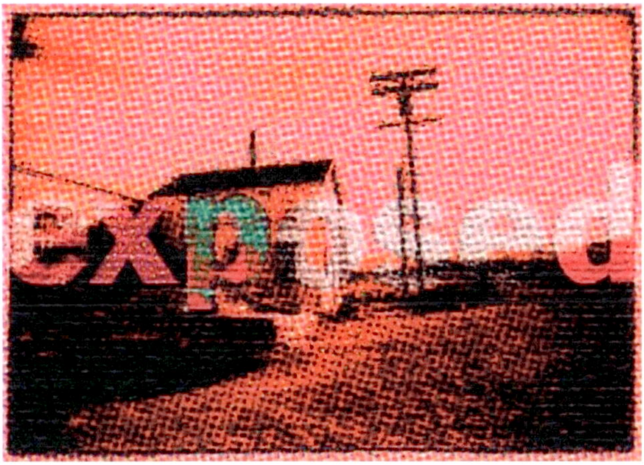

Martin S. Pribble

image for alteration

My work is primarily interested with the use and abuse of information in society, through consumer media, politics and advertising. It's the plight of modern society, that we can't escape from information that is thrust about us *en masse,* to a point where we can no longer make decisions of whether to accept the information or not. All information has an agenda and some information has worthwhile properties. Will we find it harder to filter through this information as it increases in intensity to find that which is relevant to us?

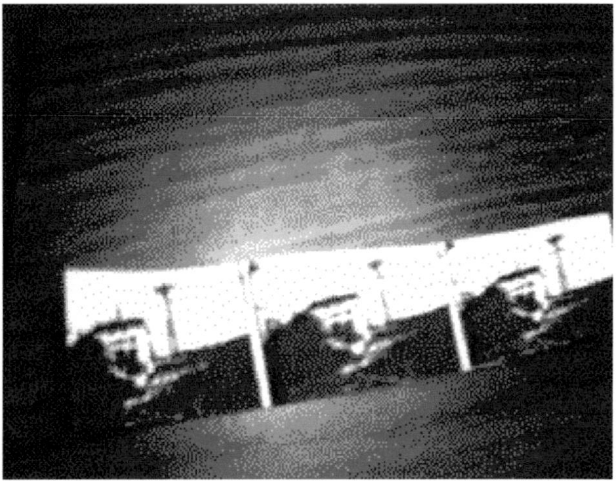

Jeremy Turner

Hray-scape

Objects and infrastructures influenced by technology are my preferred mediums.

These take the shape of:
HTML and the internet
VRML onlive worlds via fiber optic connections
Industrial Sculpture
Film/Video
Liquid Architecture
Timed Installations
Computer Music and various digitalized media.

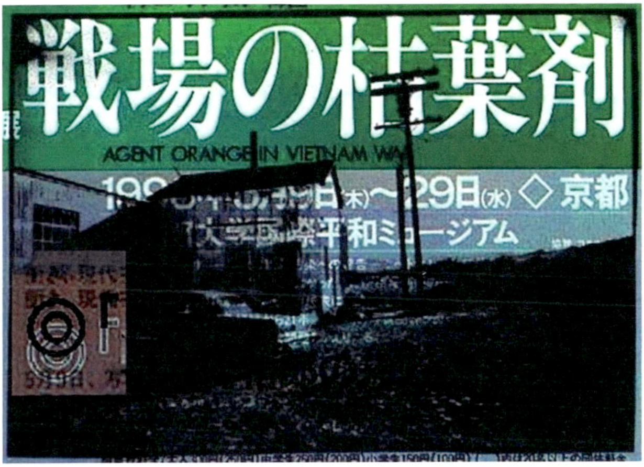

Donald Trimble

dv01 mutant

I first took the image and converted it to greyscale, then converted it into a negative image. Then I took the background image (the text part) and separated the colors. This left me with black, cyan, magenta, and yellow. Then I copied the original image and pasted it as a transparent selection. Once this was done I combined the colors back into one image. I did the small overlay of the circle inside of a circle in the foreground the same way but I decided to leave the black out of alignment.

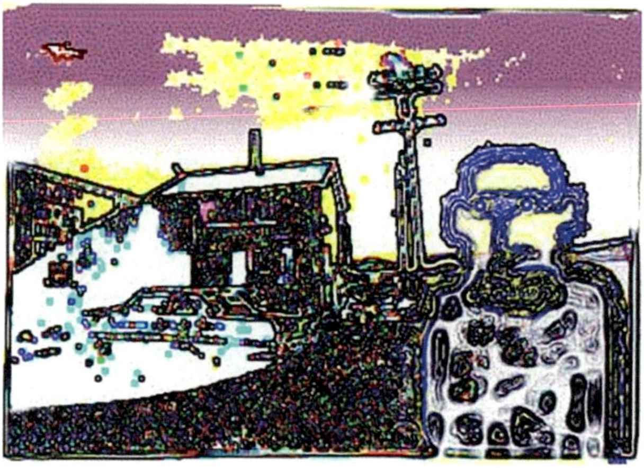

Martin Selman

digital horizon

Added a few characters found the edges and inverted a few times selected colours and that is about it.

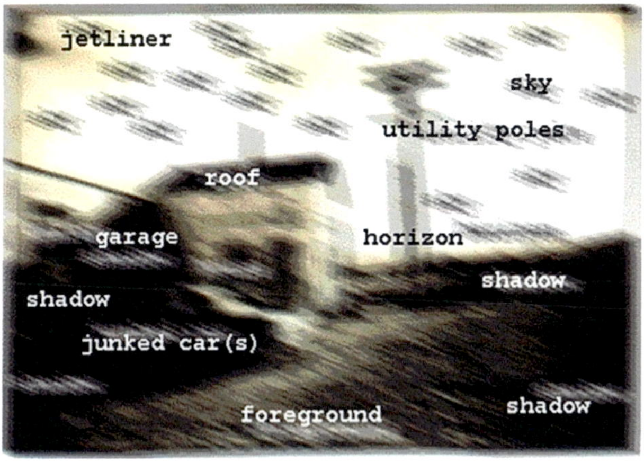

h-ray heine

Deconstruction #7

photoshop 5, death valley junction scan, retinal blur and semantic layers

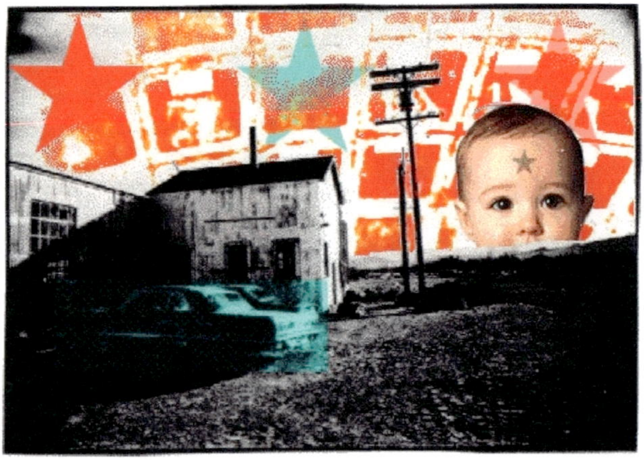

Jonathan Prince

Spectre: Born Again

Collage art with Photoshop

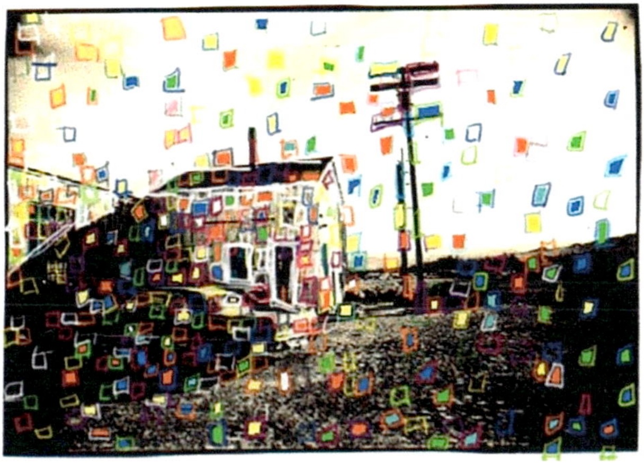

Kelly Darke

Squared

Adobe photoshop paintbrush tool and a wacom table to draw squares and fill with color.

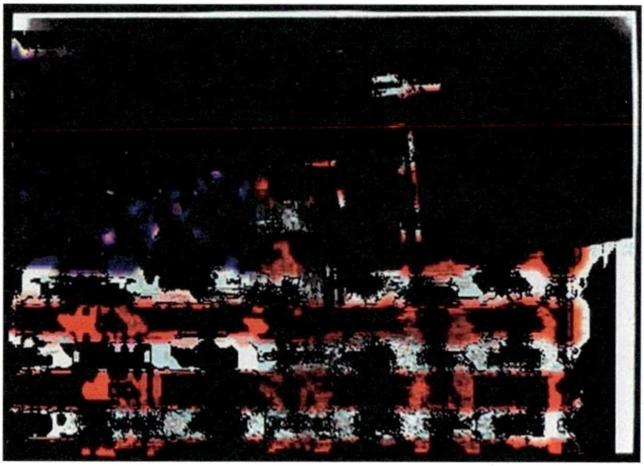

Donald Trimble

untitled

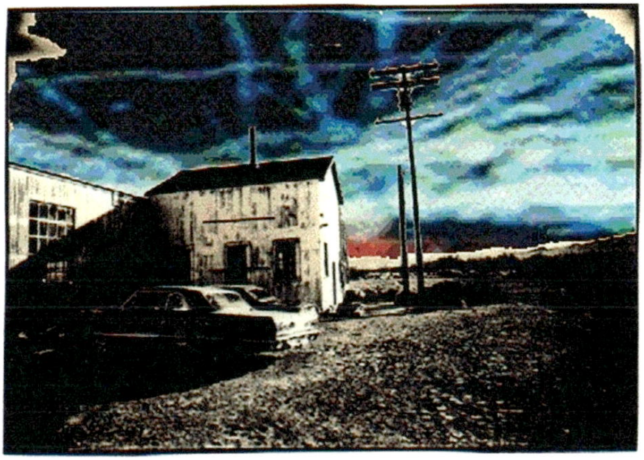

Zye Zaen

dv01 skylight

something was missing

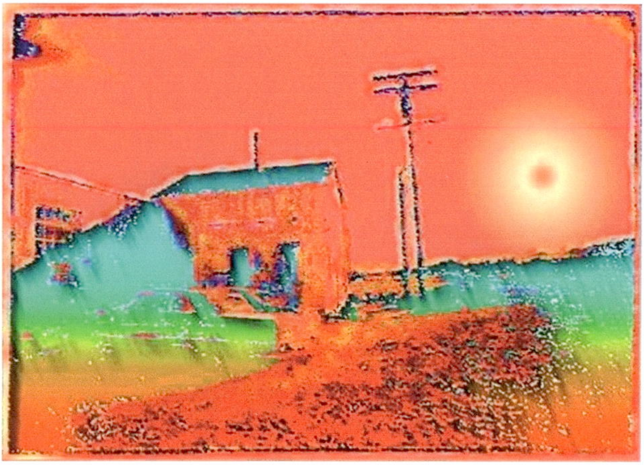

jaxun

untitled

Posterize and mask (2, 3, 4...). Make it burn people! OK, throw in the gratuitous shadow and BREATHE. OK, shake it out. Now fill, fill, composite, fill. Aaaand rest.

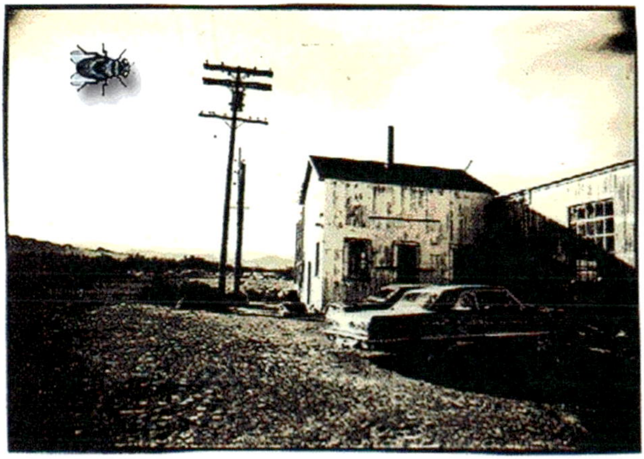

Scott Lickstein

Subjective

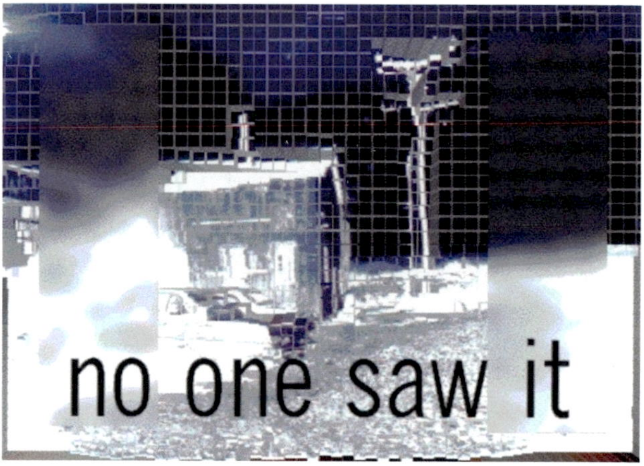

h-ray heine

dv01 deconstruction #3

Kelly Darke

Green

Adobe photoshop paintbrush tool and a wacom table to draw squares and fill with color.

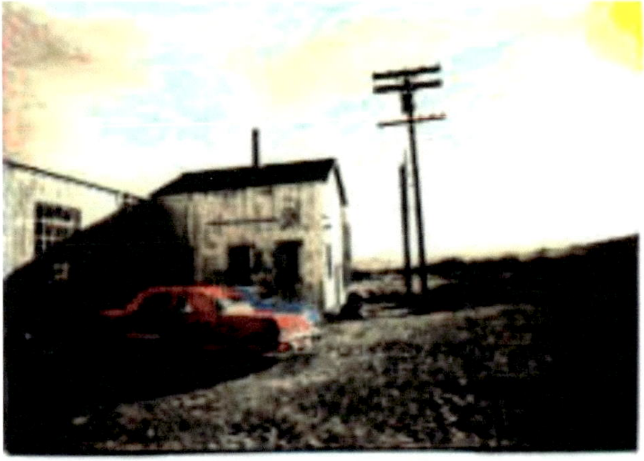

Ted Bragg

heat wave

tidied up borders, and added a few splotches of colour, but deliberately kept this to a minimum to represent the starkness of the terrain & climate.

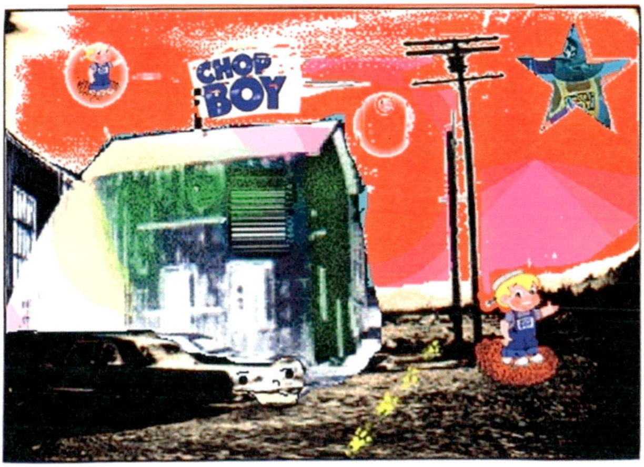

Elisha Sarti

recombinator

choreboy made me do it.

generation/mutation 1.2 online exhibition

Miquel Santos | Jean Beil | Jay Heitman | Jon Johnson | Mary Lynch | Ian Cartwright | Creepy | Ron George | Daniel C. Boyer Corey H Eiseman | Carl Patzel | Tara Camacho | Polina | H-Ray Heine Gweedo | Michael MacKenzie | Oliver Loveday | Alex McLean | E_B_A | Emily Smith | Rob Forsyth | Joe Wakefield Dmitry Misalin | Joe Keenan | Phil Smith | Stephanie Rigsby | Faith Buck | Casey Keeler | Tom R. Chambers | Udo Hanten M.G. Wood | Martin Pribble | Keith P. Chevalier | M. Marshall Kakupacal

August 2001

We don't make mistakes, just happy little accidents.

Bob Ross

v.1.2

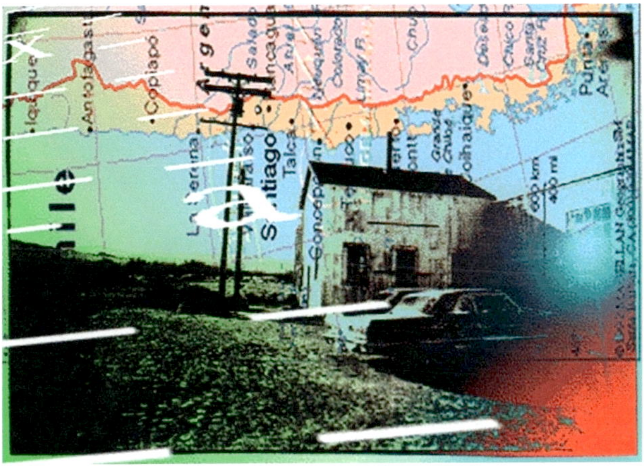

Miquel Santos

chile

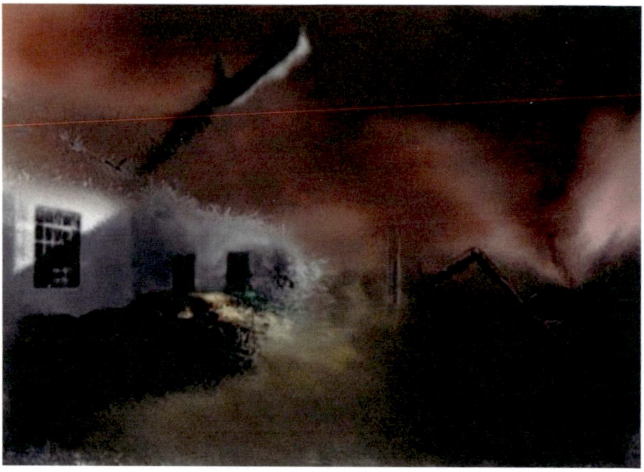

Jean Beil

Suddenly

Using Corel photo-paint8, converted from 8bit color to 24bit color, 90 dpi to 300dpi, Then I mostly painted using the common paint texture and blending brushes, keeping to the original colors from the photo dv01. Did some cut and pasting, reshaping & used An Alchemy effect on the ceiling, when finished I converted back to 100 dpi and left it in 24 bit color.

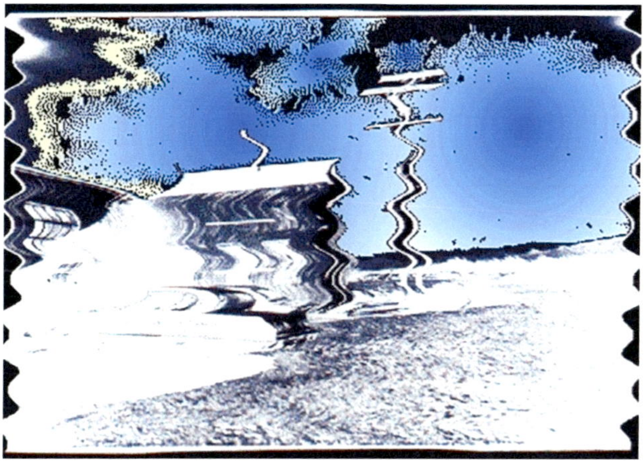

Jay Heitman

blue warp

warped in paintshop pro

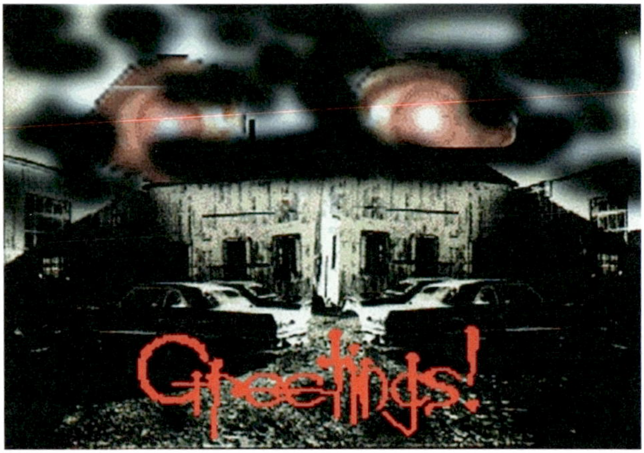

Jon Johnson

Greetings from Mars?

The image was cloned, painted, color balanced, and some collage work added into the piece to give it a "dooms-day" feel.

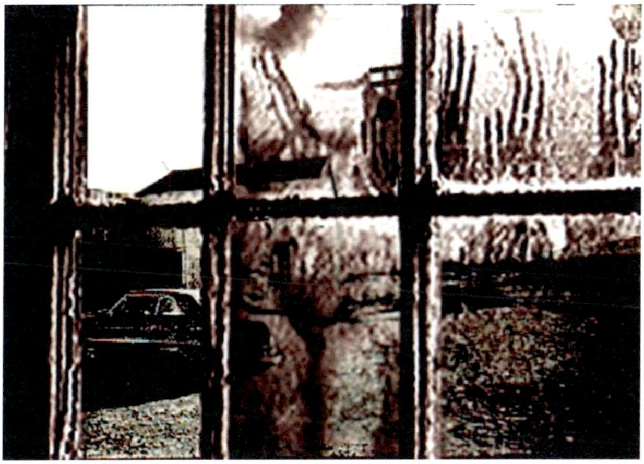

Mary Lynch

Untitled

modified with combination of window/figure layered over in Photoshop

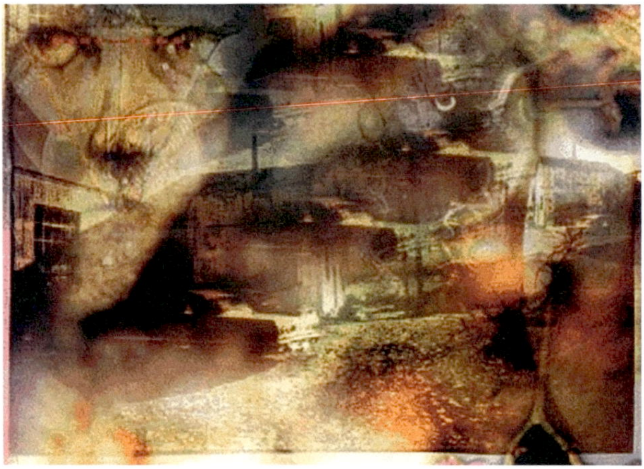

Ian Cartwright

collaborative

montage of original image & various original personal compositions

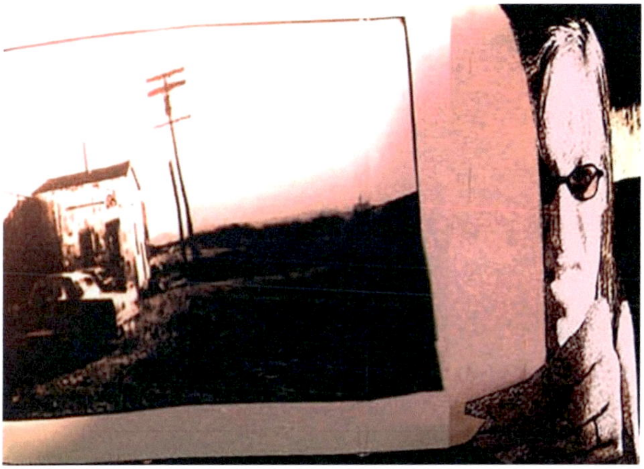

Creepy

(optional)

The original image was printed out and photographed with someone holding it, scanned into the computer and altered. The idea was to make the 2 dimensional more 3 dimensional than the actual 3 dimentional part of the image.

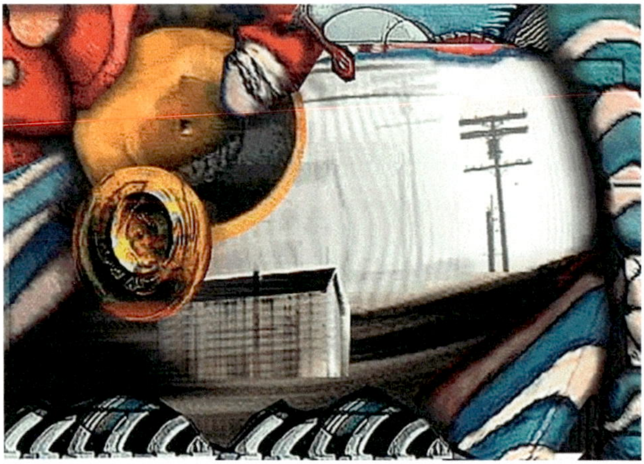

Ron George

Maximal Slide

Fauve Matisse Paint software-motion blur effect on the original; followed by some compositing of pieces of digitized paintings.

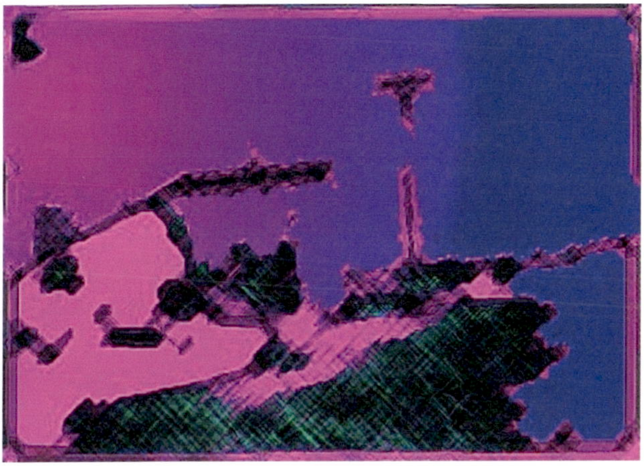

Daniel C. Boyer

The Death Mask of Justin Timberlake

made with Photoshop 5.0 using gradient, paint bucket and burn tools and colored pencil and palette knife filters

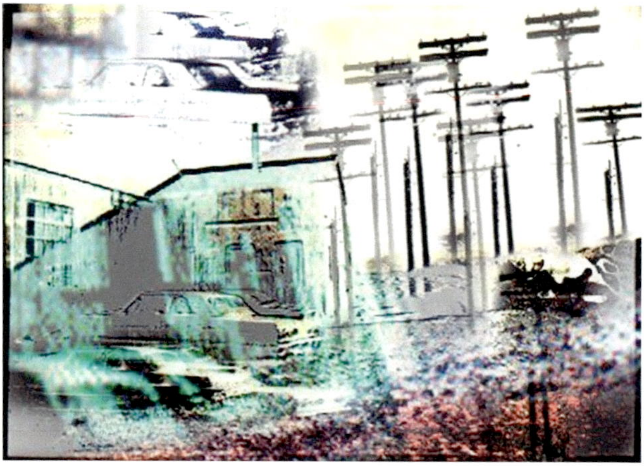

Corey H. Eiseman

apocalypse

description of modification: Mostly I kept cutting and pasting bits and pieces of the photo, adjusting the transparencies of the subsequent layers and making some of them screens or overlays. I also used the distort: glass filter once and inverted some of the layers. I don't know...it's hard to keep track once I get going.

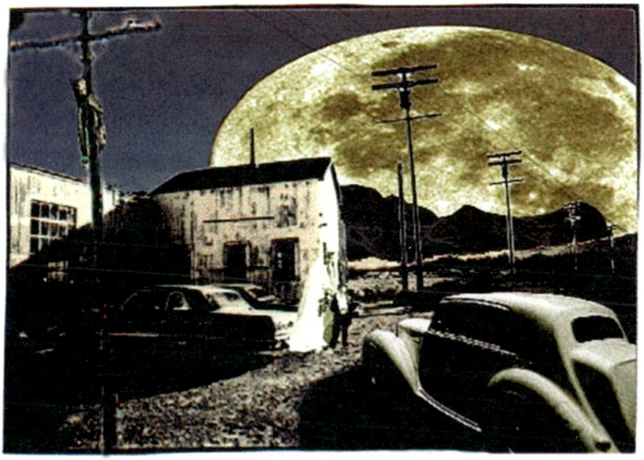

Carl Patzel

Moon Valley Wedding

I layer copied more poles; added a bear to the front one and lines with line tool. Added a Rolls Royce, a lady in a wedding dress with boy waiting for ride. Layer in moon and mountains, and adjusted colors/contrast etc. on whole scene.

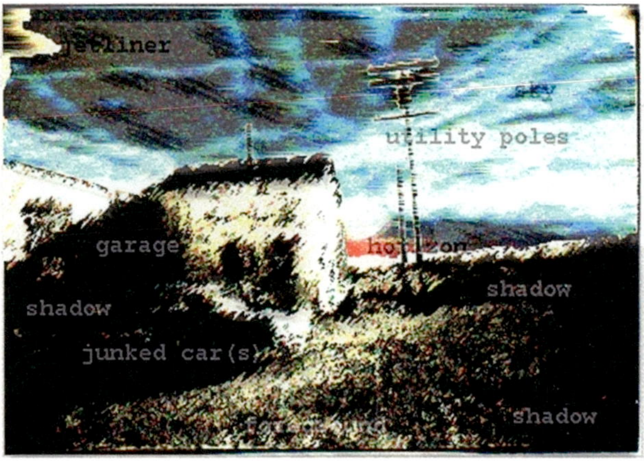

Tara Camacho

Altered State

By taking several of the other images I used the overlay technique to create the new image. This is truly collaborative work.

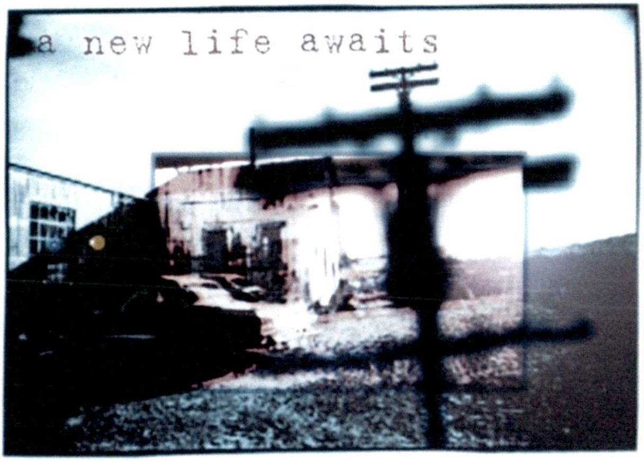

Polina

a new life

leaving early in the morning for something new.

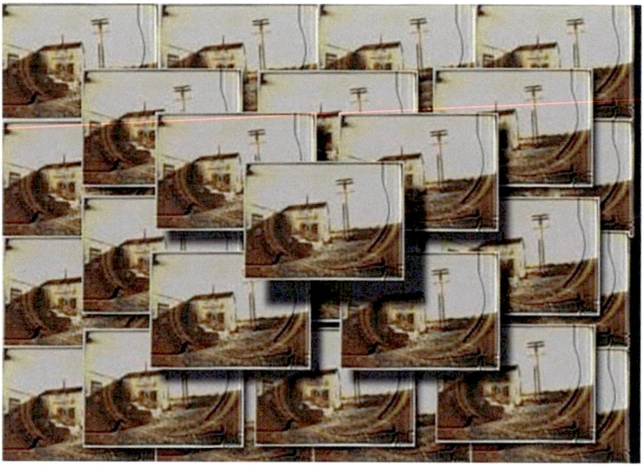

H-Ray Heine

multiply (retinal)

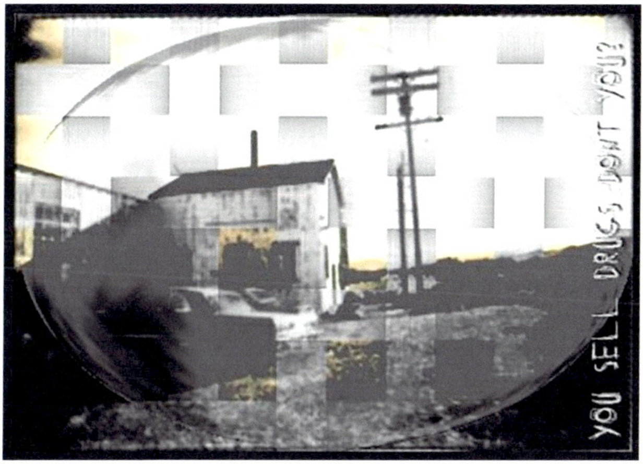

gweedo

kansas 72

Ps5-layers, masks, filters

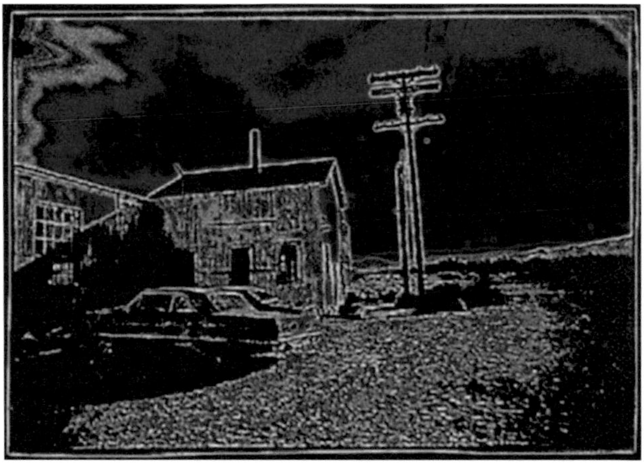

Michael MacKenzie

Nightscape

Accented edges in highlighted areas after adjusting hue.

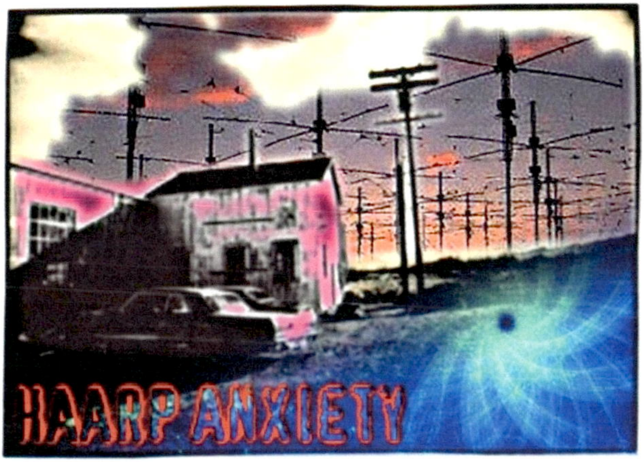

Oliver Loveday

HAARP Anxiety

HAARP Anxiety relates to the on-going project the US military is doing use low frequency radio signals to communicate with submarines. It also affects weather patterns and human cognition. A little mix of the HAARP structure with a fractal is my response to that anxiety.

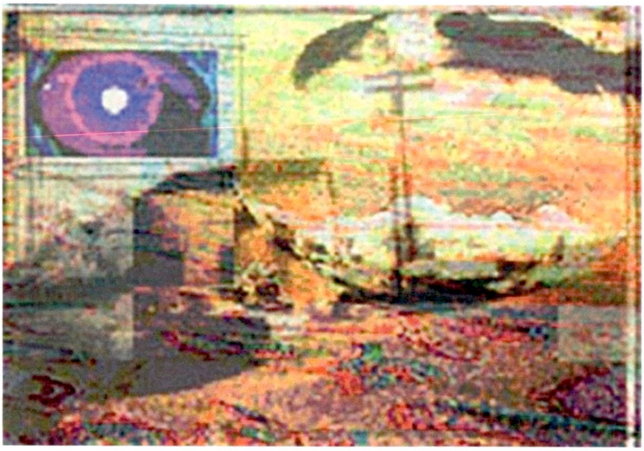

Alex McLean

untitled

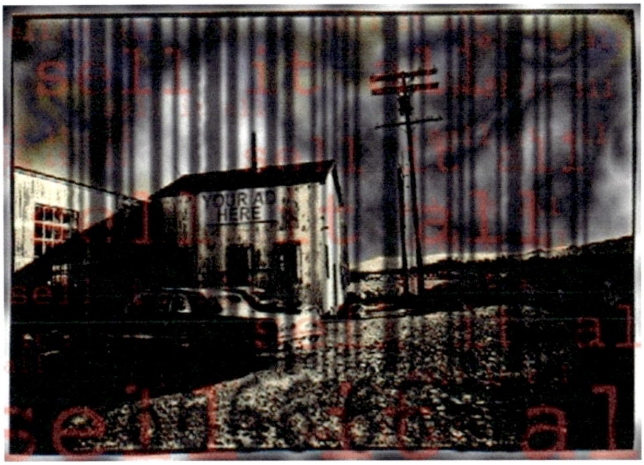

E_B_A

sell it all

First, I created layers for my new text ("sell it all") and the barcode graphic (which was severely altered). Then, I worked on changing the sky until I found the desired asthetic. I proceeded to apply a picture of myself in the lower-right corner (it's there- trust me) because, hey - I'm a selfish bastard and I hafta put my mug in everything...anyway... next, I applied the sign, and began adjusting the various transparancies of my layers. I also applied what I referred to as the frame (the white area around the photo). Finally, after a little tweaking... voila! A statement about society (and not a very subtle one at that).

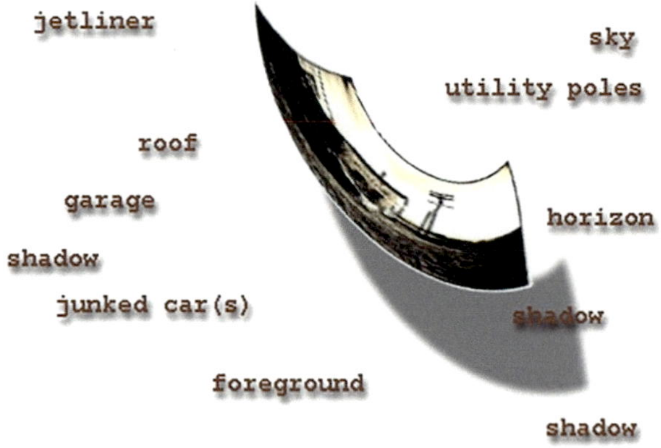

H-Ray Heine

deconstruction #13

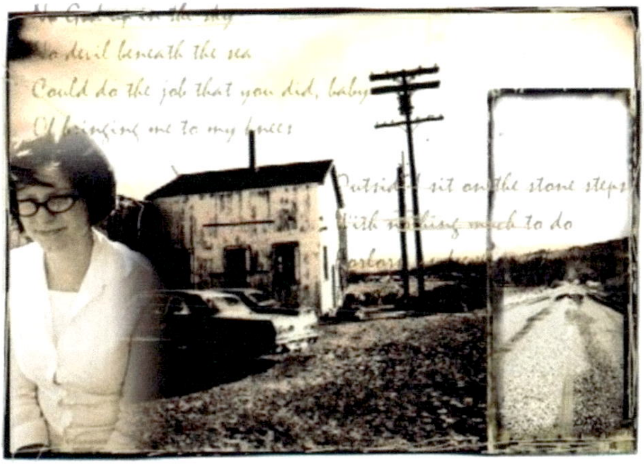

Emily Smith

Aubreii

Opened this baby up in Photoshop 5.0 and 9 layers later…

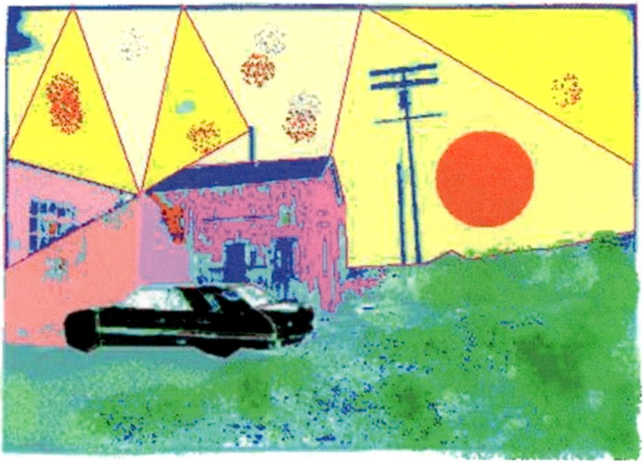

Rob Forsyth

mutation

I loaded the file into microsoft photo editor and adjusted the brightness and contrast then I saved the file as a bmp file and loaded it into microsoft paint. I then divided it up into using the line tool and added different colour fills to the separate areas and a bit of filling in with the spray can. I opened the bmp file in photo editor again and softened it a touch and saved it as a jpg.

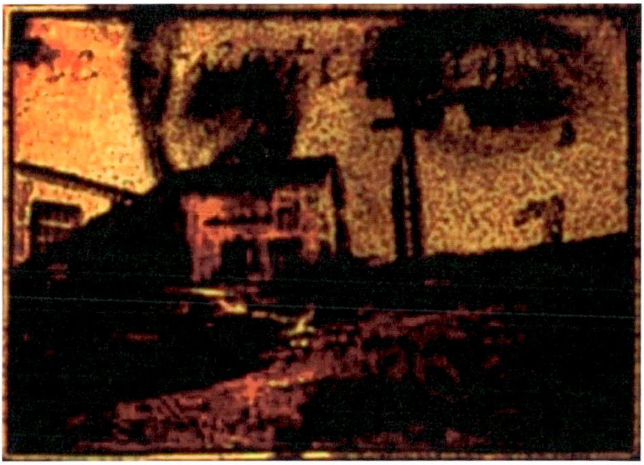

Joe Wakefield

he's watching

Using Paint Shop Pro I layered in my face and some text, and then repeatedly sharpened and blurred the images and finally overlayed some color.

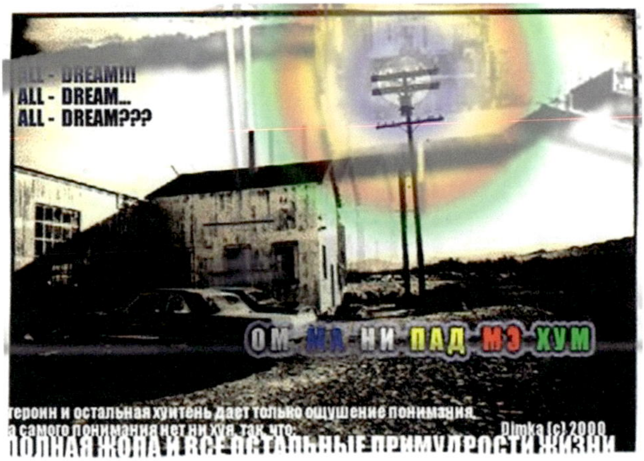

Dmitry Misalin

all – dream!.../?

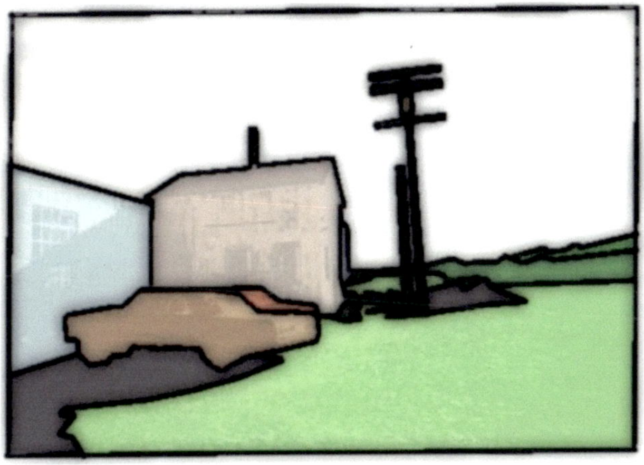

Joe Keenan

Generific

I've modified a couple of other pictures this way... what I call 'generifying'...first time I've tried it on the computer... added the gaussian blur outlines, and left the original picture in the background to enhance......

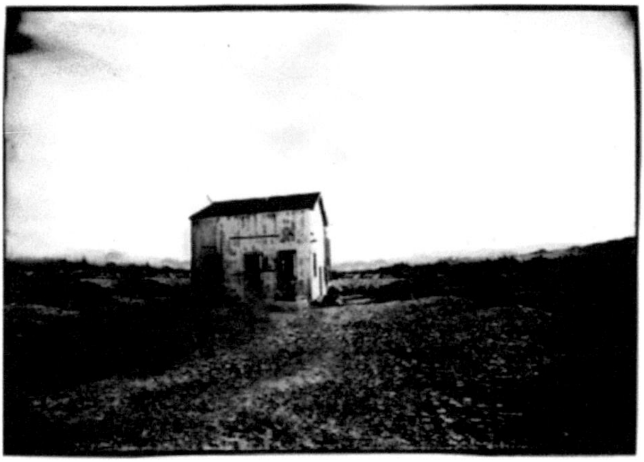

Phil Smith

Untitled

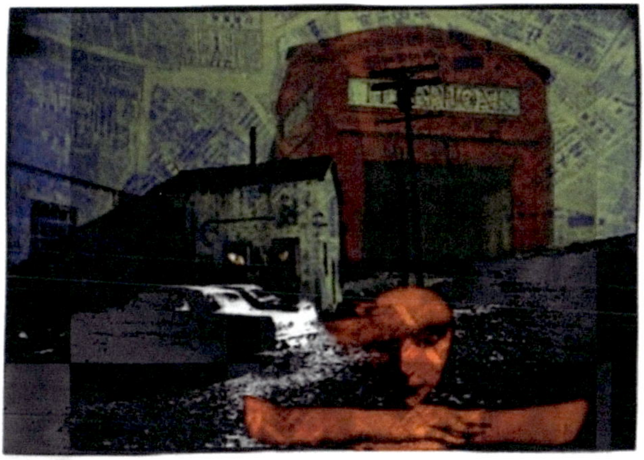

Stephanie Rigsby

mutation

mutation: incorporation and tweaking of photographs taken by myself – if you're looking for more specifics do ask.

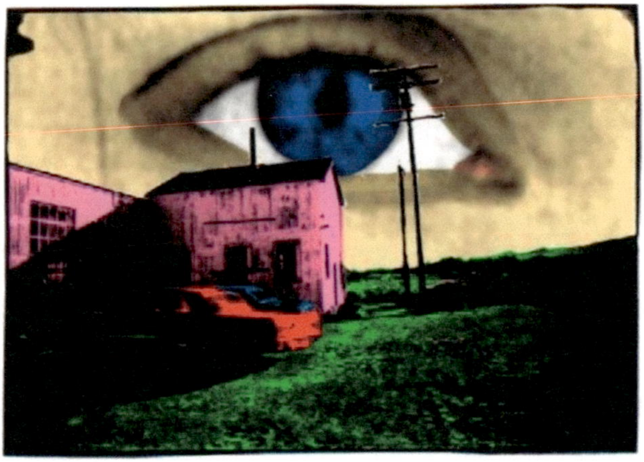

Faith Buck

Whether I

It seemed the obvious thing to do

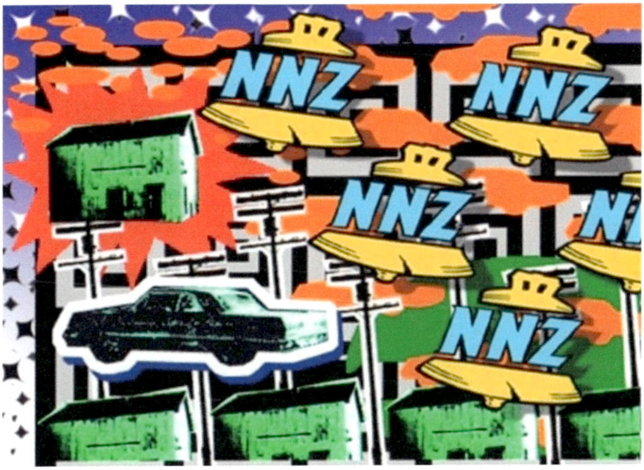

Casey Keeler

Ergonomicon's Response to Infinity

Techniques: Photoshop, stolen/contaminated images from the web, slice n' dice/shake and bake.

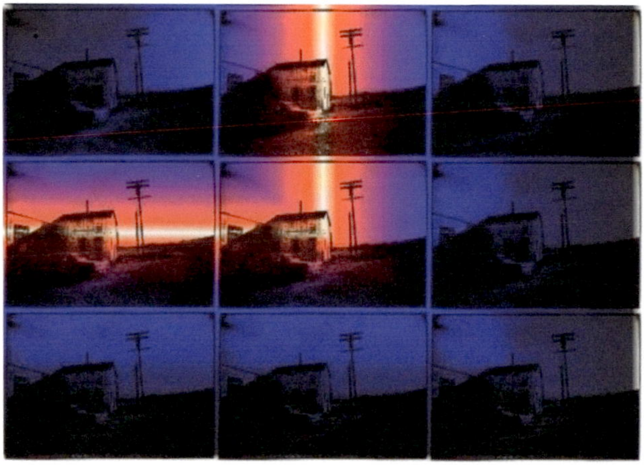

Tom R. Chambers

Alteration dv01a

Corel Photo—Paint 7/tile/KPT Gradient

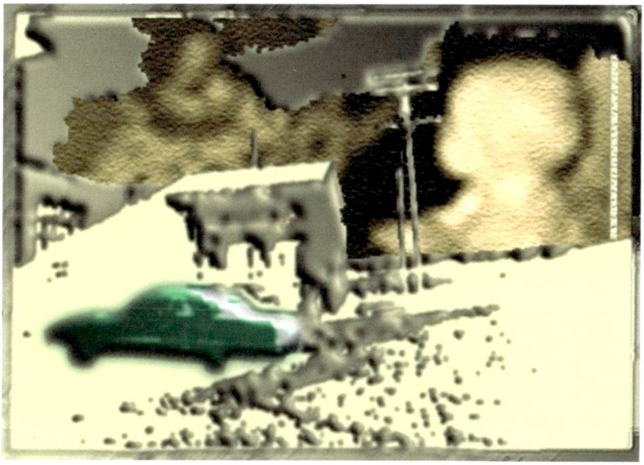

Udo Hanten

boy Zone

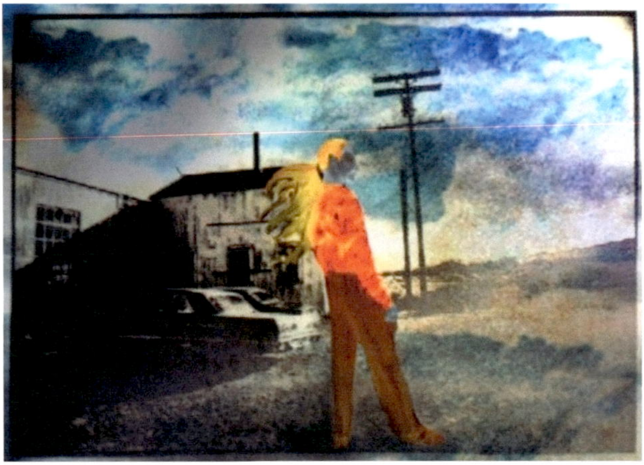

M.G. Wood

none

I used Painter to create this, with layers and painting textures under the layers.

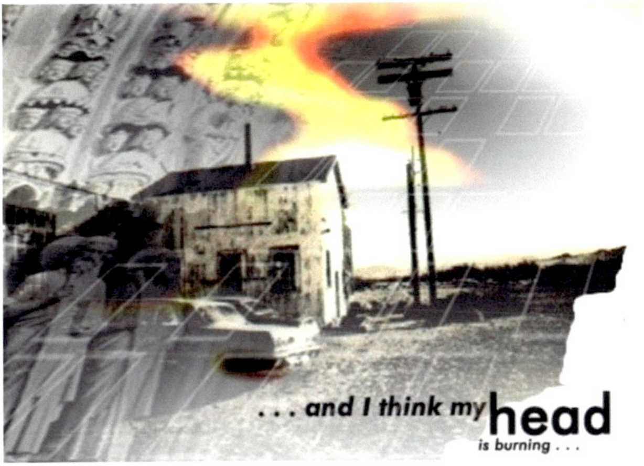

Martin Pribble

The Mercy Seat

"The Mercy Seat" inspired by Johnny Cash's version of the Nick Cave song.

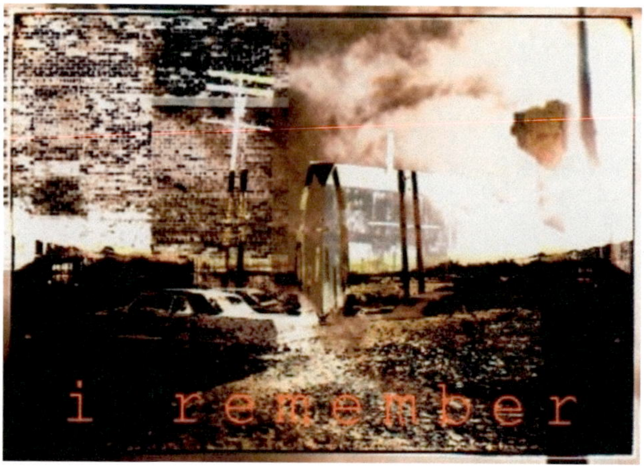

Keith P Chevalier

i remember

Using Photoshop, I merged various images to create the layers that I think add to a sort of depth that attempts to stay within the original image system.

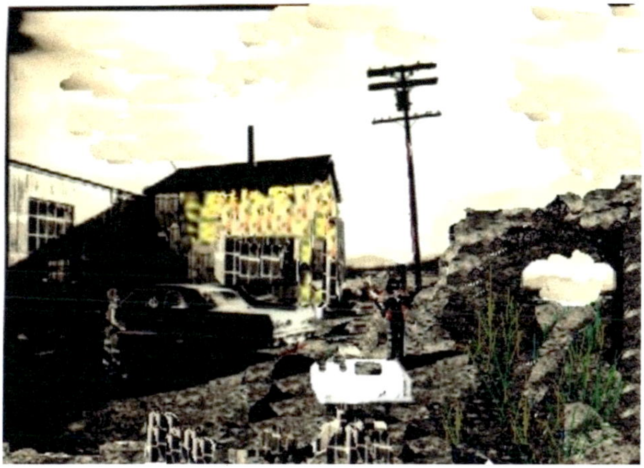

M Marshall

the last yard sale

modification: primarily with clone tool and color

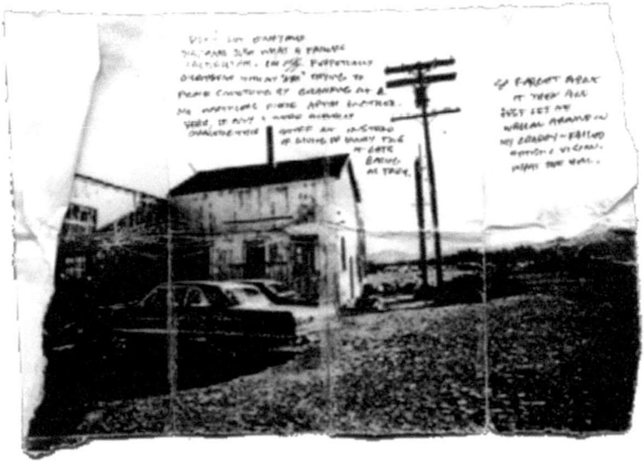

Kakupacal

untitled

no title...no pretentious "explanations" of the deep artistic techniques and meanings behind them; just goofing around.

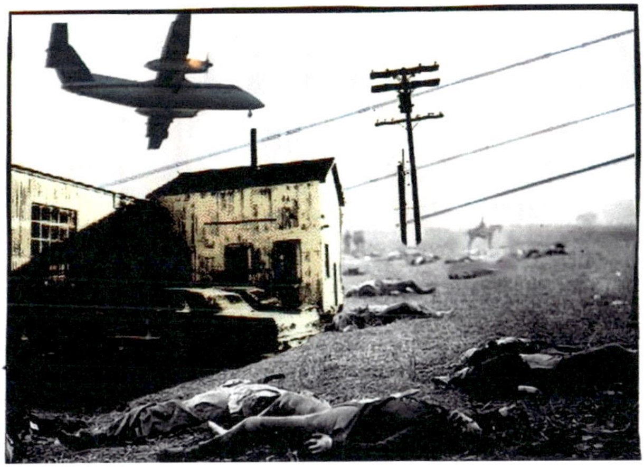

Anonymous

untitled

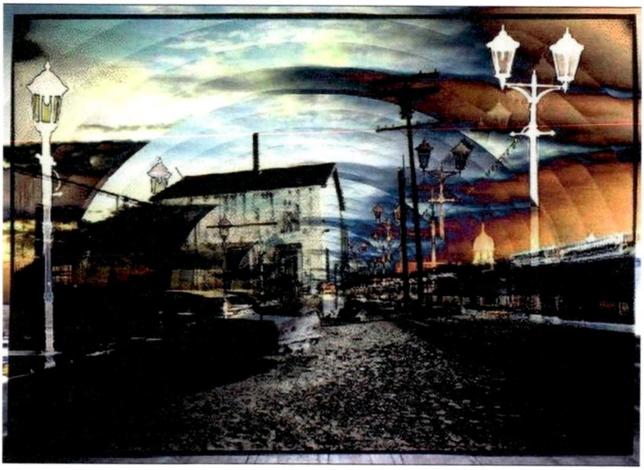

Anonymous

untitled

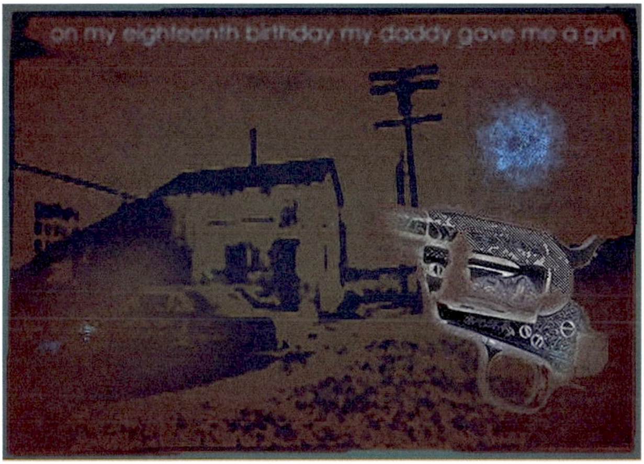

Anonymous

untitled

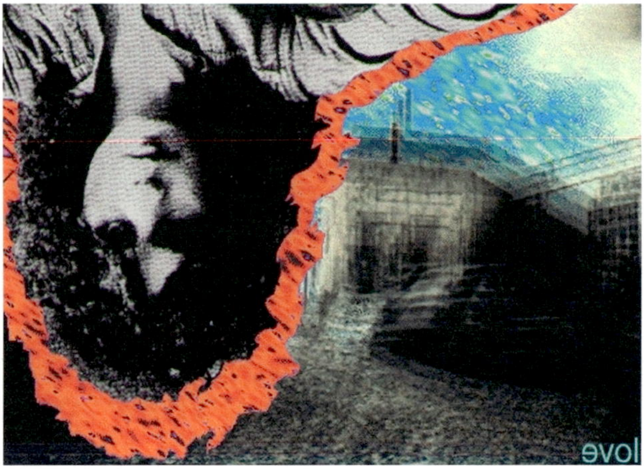

Anonymous

Bolan

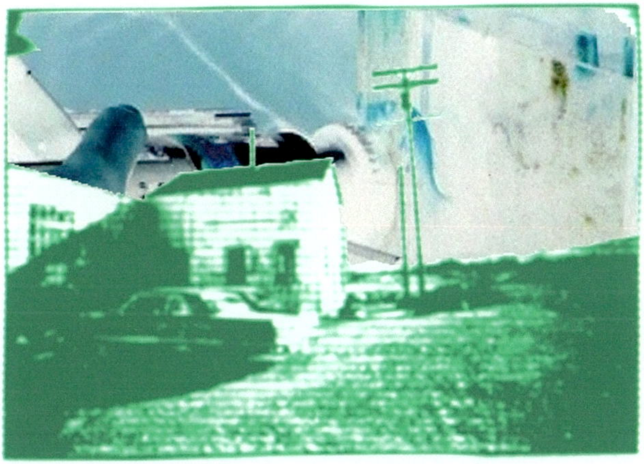

Udo Hanten

Fish waiting 4 water

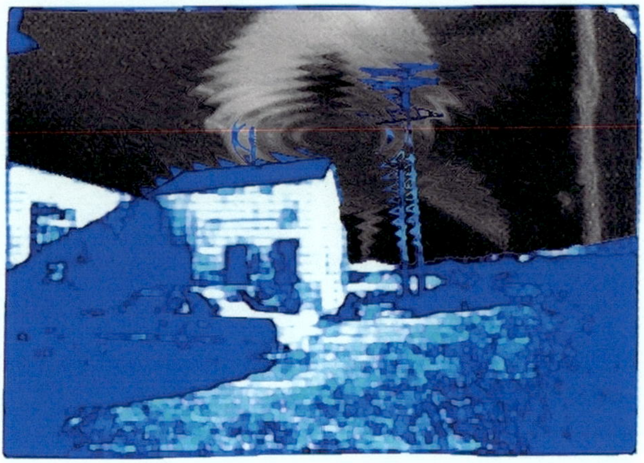

Udo Hanten

Fishcar

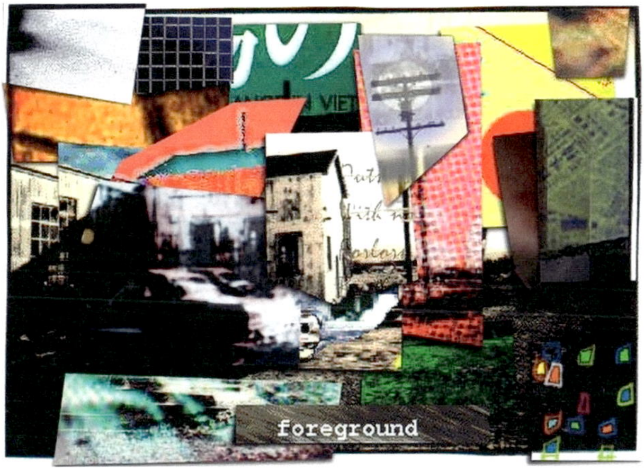

Kakupacal

untitled

2.0 Machines

Soon after the introduction of Google Street View (GSV) service in 2007, the iconic Street View cars with their nine-eyed cameras on the roof began to visit increasingly remote areas of the country, including Southern California's Mojave Desert (Google 2020).[1] There, one of the places visited by Street View cars was Death Valley Junction, an unincorporated community in Inyo County, California, at the inter-section of State Road 190 and State Road 127, with an official population of less than four (Wikipedia 2018). The seed image of generation/mutation, the shot of an abandoned car repair shop somewhere in the desert, had been taken there in 1981.

Death Valley Junction lies near the center of a triangle formed by three locations of the American West that have left a mark on popular culture: the "secret" Area 51 to the North, glittering Las Vegas to the East and, to the South, Barker Ranch, Charles Manson's last hiding place before his arrest.

The deserts of the America West attract photographers, painters, philosophers, psychopaths, hermits, and an endless stream of tourists in minivans, campers, and SUV's. In my case, it was the fascination with the landscape of Southern California deserts that attracted me the most. But the reason for my visit to Death Valley Junction in 1981 goes back some months before I left my home in Germany to move to California. Friends at the local city theater, the Stadt Theater Krefeld, told me about this amazing place somewhere in the Southern California desert. It was basically a road junction surrounded by miles and miles of desert. The main businesses there were a diner, a car repair shop, and a gas station. The settlement was part of a world where 'Next gas 63 miles' signs warn travelers that they are about to leave the safety and comforts of air-conditioned life behind as they drive out into the desert. In the beginning, it may have been an old mining town of sorts, with a railroad perhaps. In more recent times, after WW II, a handful of people managed to live there, but when the oil crisis hit in the seventies, causing gas shortages, travel restrictions, and price hikes, visitor traffic to the remote Southern California desert died out overnight and the place became a modern ghost town.[2]

But even more fascinating was the story about a classical ballet dancer who supposedly had settled in Death Valley Junction. She had taken over the abandoned "opera" building of the town and performed daily—often to an empty house—pieces of classical ballet in this virtual ghost town somewhere in the desert. According to the story, she even went so far and painted an audience on the walls of the theatre.[3] Can there be a more poetic gesture?

Unfortunately, I did not meet Marta Becket on my visit to Death Valley Junction. At the time, I did not even know if the story was true. This was, after all, many years before the

Internet, not to mention Smartphone or GPS. The place was empty, no one around. The diner was boarded up. Inside, on the counter and stools, everything was covered evenly with a thin layer of eggshell colored dust, making it look like a modern art installation that, appropriately enough, was left abandoned in the desert. Across the street from the diner is the old service station and garage, where I took the photograph that later became the seed image for *generation/mutation.* The two cars parked on the side looked like they might still run. In the middle of the square formed by the u-shaped Mexican-Colonial style adobe buildings stood the partially stripped fuselage of a small airplane, a Cessna 172 perhaps. At the far end of the square was the Amargosa Opera House, the stage for Marta Becket's ballet performances. It was late morning and the whole place seemed to get hotter and dryer by the minute. And not a soul in sight. I took some photographs and soon got back in the car and left.

In 1981, It took hours of desert driving to get to Death Valley Junction. A quarter of a century later, in 2007, anyone with Internet access could explore the desert town in Street View with just a few clicks on the keyboard.

Furthermore, zooming into a section of one of the Street View images produces a close approximation of the scene captured in the original image. Naturally, there are many differences. The two cars in front of the building in the original photograph are long gone. The angle of the shadows indicates that the Street View image was taken earlier in the day. And, among many other details, a fence now appears to separate the scene of the original picture from the position of the Street View car on California State Road 127.

But despite the differences, the two images show one and the same location. The two main buildings and the utility poles on the right are virtually unchanged in both pictures. Apparently, the buildings and utility poles made it largely unscathed through the twenty-five years of desert climate that separate the two images.

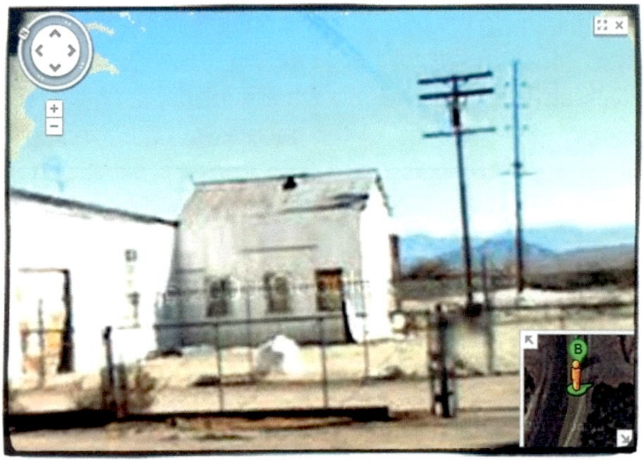

Death Valley Junction, California. Google Street View (2008) screenshot placed behind *generation/mutation* seed image frame

The availability of the Google-made images of the same location in 2008 raised important and completely unexpected questions for the first, entirely human-sourced version of *generation/mutation*. Could the Street View images of the location in Death Valley Junction be valid contributions to the project? Are they instances of a new type of readymade—a digital readymade—that, like its more famous predecessors, simply needed to be found and declared to be a readymade work? Are these Google-mades not only the equivalent of found objects in the digital domain, but also the raw and ready material for a series of exclusively machine-sourced images, produced by an enormous, automatic, global digital recording machine?

Each of the human-made contributions of *generation/ mutation v.1.0* presents a very personal interpretation of the location depicted—mediated by the image and its manipulations. Each contribution develops a unique, subjective way of seeing and, in many cases, of changing the look of the location altogether. Each involves work, a creative engagement by each artist with the raw material provided by the seed image.

The machine-made images occupy the opposite side of the spectrum as far as subjective and personal expression is concerned. They are completely impersonal, mechanical, automatically generated scans. The scanned images in turn are constitutive parts of a much larger product generated by the digital mapping machine. Some of the GSV images of the location in Death Valley Junction include detail areas that could be considered visually "equivalent" to the original seed image, but are these images a new type of *alteration of the original image*?

The GSV images are not manipulations of the seed image's JPEG file as envisioned by the original project instructions. But they do offer a unique way of seeing and representing the appearance of a physical location—a Street View style of seeing the exact same place that was captured in the original photograph decades earlier.

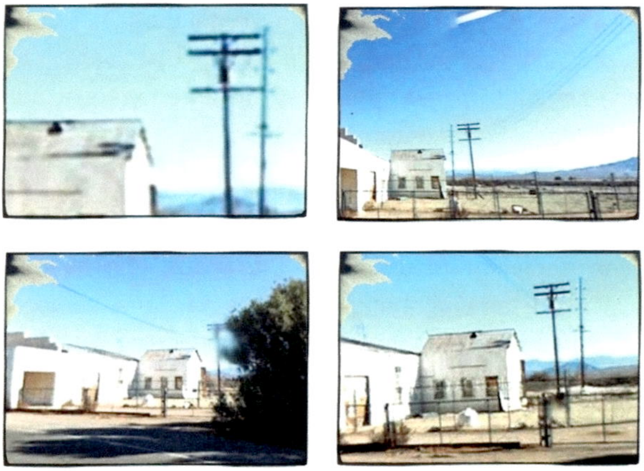

Selection 3: Google Street View images included in *generation/mutation* v. 2.1

Of course, there is no "author" or "photographer" in the traditional sense. There is no "decisive moment" in which a scan had to be taken. Instead, the images are generated by a giant digital automaton; they are the work of a machine.

The Google-made images included in this second phase of *generation/mutation* work perfectly as digital readymades.[4] They present alterations of the way in which the place shown on the original photograph is rendered and represented in a digital universe. As a group, the images make up an enigmatic collection of machine-sourced contributions to the project, *generation/mutation v.2*.

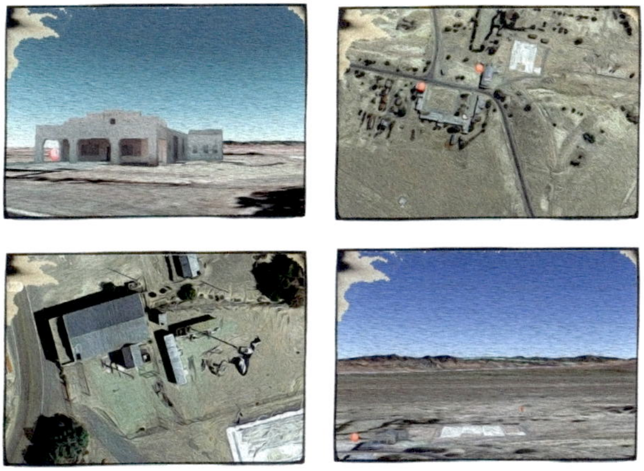

Selection 4: Google Earth images included in *generation/mutation* v. 2.2

Version 2.1 of consists of a selection of Google Street View images, version 2.2 presents images found on Google Earth. To indicate their role as contributions to the project, the images were placed behind the frame of the original seed image. Apart from some cropping and placement within the frame, the Street View images in version 2.1 are shown exactly as they were found—readymade—in GSV, without alterations or enhancements.

The second selection of contributions, *generation/mutation* 2.2, is entirely sourced from Google Earth images and the images received some minor digital enhancements. Specifically, the application of an "oil-painting" filter gives the machine-generated images a new visual style, making the photographic images look like traditional oil paintings with a less traditional subject matter—satellite images.[5]

Not all parts of Google Earth images are purely photographic reproductions of what can be seen on the ground. Several of the images include architectural enhancements in the rendering of the two buildings in the center of the original seed image. The 3-D features enhance the orthodox photographic rendering of the location by inserting an AI-generated 3-D version of the building structure. Google's architecture feature builds a virtual model of the building at a given location, enhancing its defining features, and placing them into the location imagery in place of a photographic rendering of the buildings at the location. These architectural enhancements contained in the Google-made images present the viewer with a new type of visual map of the world, an *augmented* reality, a hyperreal depiction of the real and original location.

Notes

[1] The first area to be mapped consisted of only a few blocks in Palo Alto, California. The classic Google Street View car with its cameras mounted on the roof were deployed to generate the initial scans of the area and—ultimately—the initial data for the services. To expand the areas accessible to Street View, Google added different cameras and mounts, each designed for specific terrains and purposes. In addition to the by now iconic Street View car with its nine-eyed cameras mounted on the roof, Google added the Street View Trekker, where the cameras are fixed to a backpack which is carried by a hiker. The Trekker made it possible for Street View to include trails in and around the Grand Canyon and other areas accessible only by foot. A Street View Trolley was specifically designed for smooth scans of museums and other indoor spaces like the White House. A Street View Snowmobile was made for arctic areas with snow-covered terrains that are inaccessible to other vehicle types and, finally, Google Street View developed a Three-Wheeler, ideal for the exploration of cities with small and narrow streets. (Google 2020)

[2] Death Valley Junction started as a company town owned by the Pacific Coast Borax Company. It was built in 1923-24. Originally named Amargosa ("bitter water" in Payute), the mining company renamed the place Death Valley Junction after the railroad junction nearby. The center of the town is a u-shaped complex of Mexican Colonial-style adobe buildings that include a 23-room hotel and the Amargosa Opera House (Wikipedia 2018). Both locations were used in David Lynch's 1997 motion picture *Lost Highway.* The movie's "lost highway" is California State Road 127, which runs

through Death Valley Junction, and the "Lost Highway Hotel" in the film is the Amargosa Hotel (Wikipedia 2020).

[3] The ballet dancer my friends had told me about was the legendary Marta Becket, who had settled in Death Valley Junction in 1967 and performed in the Amargosa Opera House. Todd Robinson's documentary about Marta Becket, Amargosa (2000), chronicles her life and work (Wikipedia 2020).

[4] They also are very different objects compared to Marcel Duchamp's original conception and performative practice. See pp. below for a more detailed discussion.

[5] Traditional oil paintings with motifs taken from satellite and aerial imagery is an established genre in today's artworld. The generation/mutation v.2.2 contributions are fakes in the sense that they are not actual oil paintings but merely digital manipulations of satellite imagery.

generation/mutation 2.1

machine sourced contributions

2008 - 2012

A map is not the territory it represents, but, if correct, it has a similar structure to the territory, which accounts for its usefulness.

—Alfred Korzybski, "Science and Sanity"

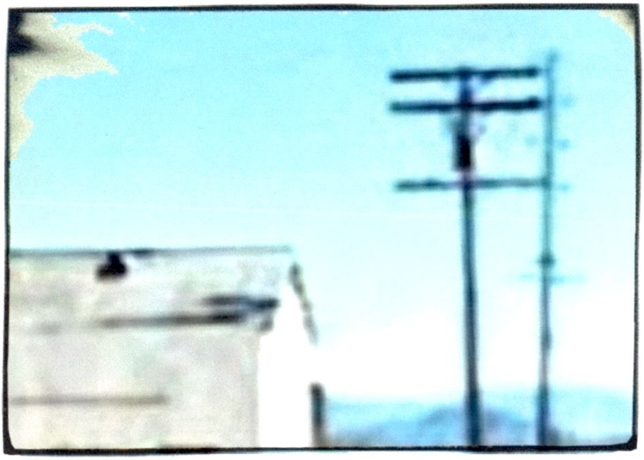

Google-made 200801

DVJ retinal

Detail of Google Street View image (2008).

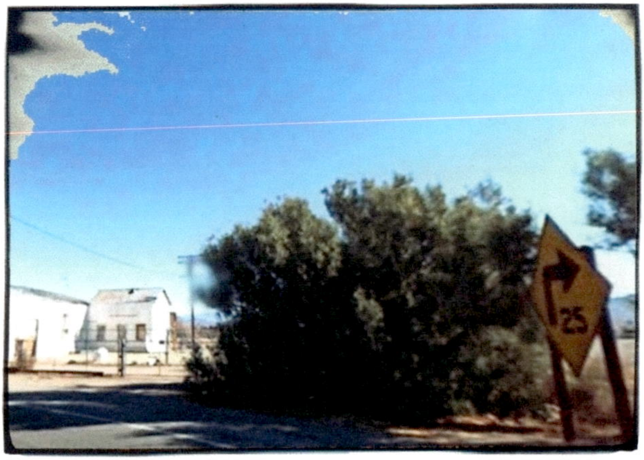

Google-made 200802

DVJ bend 25

Google Street View screenshot.

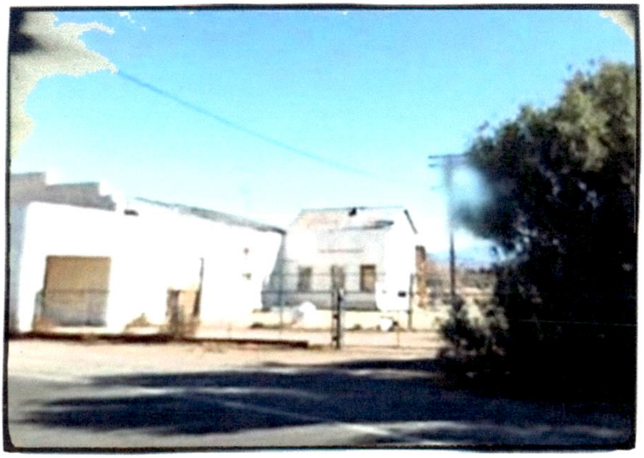

Google-made 200803

DVJ drive by postcard

Google Street View screenshot

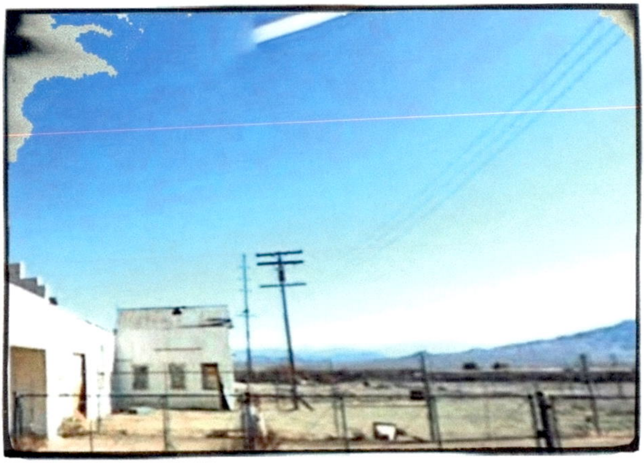

Google-made 200804

DVJ blue sky

Google Street View screenshot.

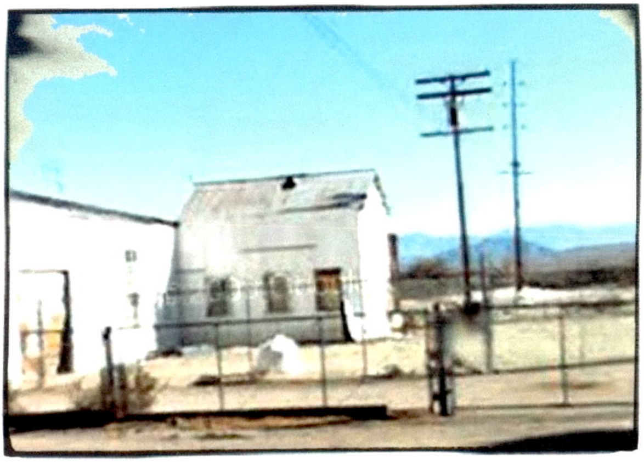

Google-made 200805

DVJ deja vu

Google Street View screenshot.

generation/mutation 2.2

a selection of machine sourced contributions based on

Google Earth images

digitally enhanced by H-Ray Heine

2008 - 2012

In time, those Unconscionable Maps no longer satisfied, and the Cartographers Guilds struck a Map of the Empire whose size was that of the Empire, and which coincided point for point with it. The following Generations, who were not so fond of the Study of Cartography as their Forebears had been, saw that that vast Map was Useless, and not without some Pitilessness was it, that they delivered it up to the Inclemencies of Sun and Winters.

Jorge Luis Borges, "On Exactitude in Science"

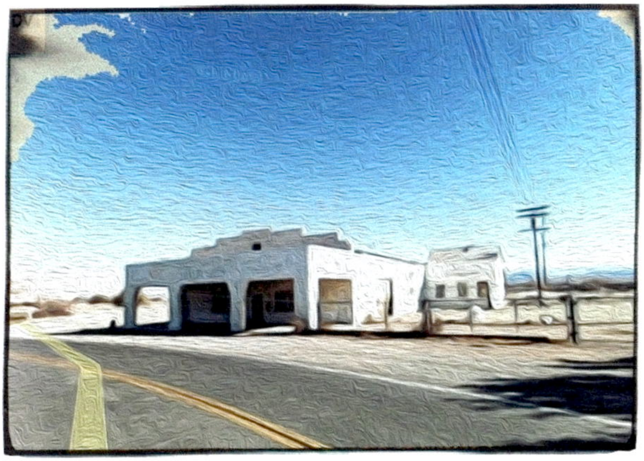

Topos 200806

Death Valley Junction (Google-made)

2008 Google Earth image with color enhancements and oil painting surface simulation.

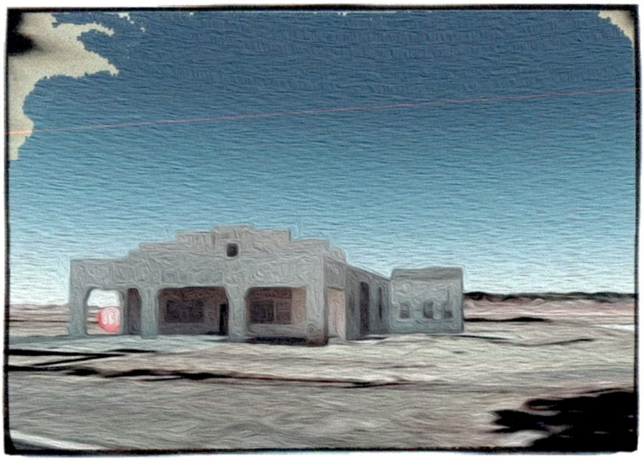

Topos 200801

Death Valley Junction

2008 Google Earth image with color enhancements and oil painting surface simulation. Architecture enhancement. Omission of telephone poles and wires, fencing on the right side of the main building, but the shadows from the bushes on the right are kept.

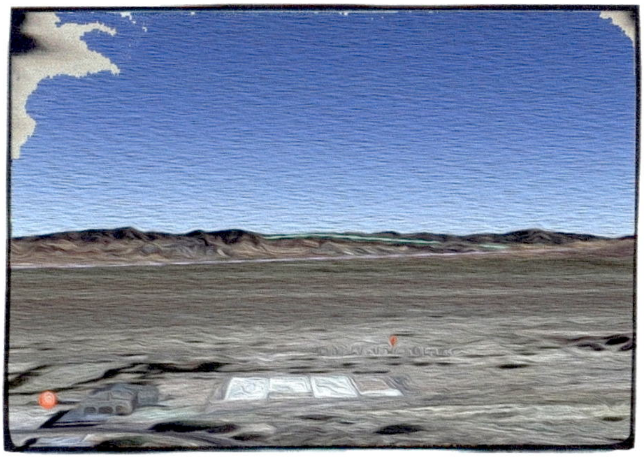

Topos 200802

Death Valley Junction

2008 Google Earth image with color enhancements and oil painting surface simulation.

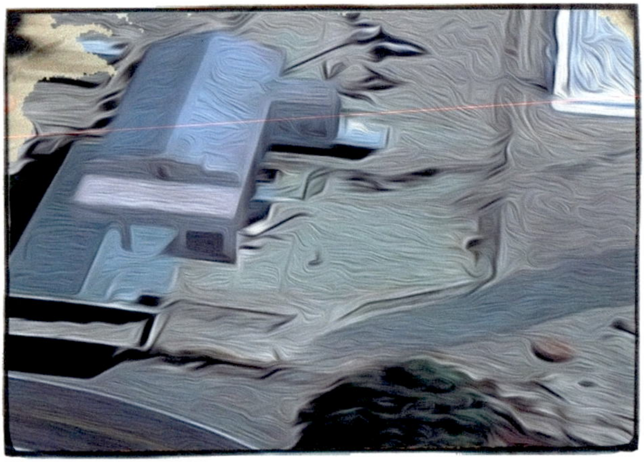

Topos 200800

Death Valley Junction

2008 Google Earth image with color enhancements and oil painting surface simulation.

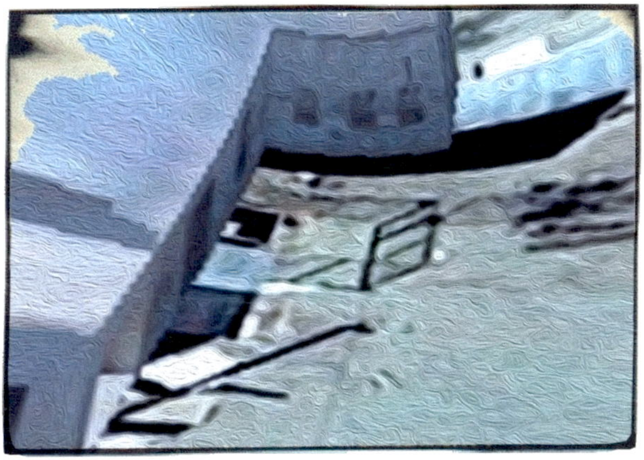

Topos 200805

Death Valley Junction

2008 Google Earth image with color enhancements and oil painting surface simulation.

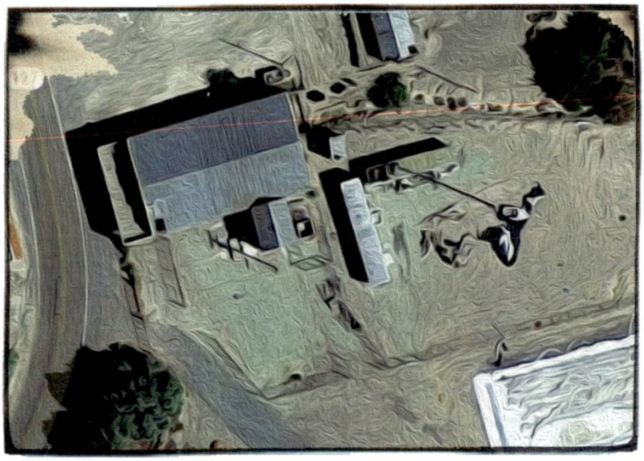

Topos 200804

Death Valley Junction

2008 Google Earth image with color enhancements and oil painting surface simulation.

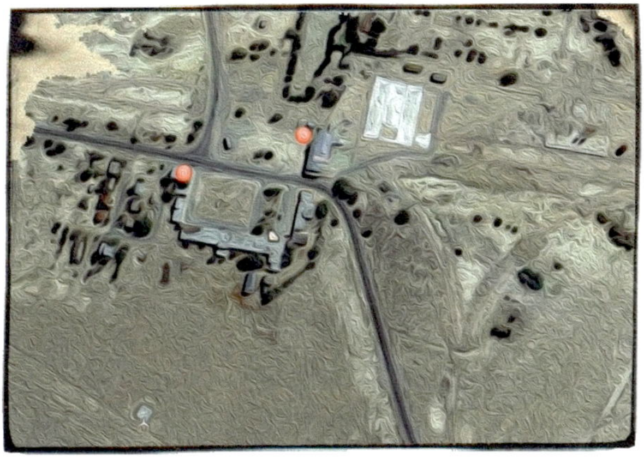

Topos 200803

Death Valley Junction

2008 Google Earth image with color enhancements and oil painting surface simulation.

3.0 Simulators

An entirely new type of contributions to *generation/mutation* became available in 2018 – images based on the project's original seed image, but transformed by neural style transfer (NST) algorithms. Neural style transfer applications make it possible for computers to "learn" the painting style that is encoded in an image file of a painting, the style image, and then to apply that style to the content of another image file, the content image, to generate its output, the result image. The AI-generated image tends to look like a visual hybrid of the two source images, the style and content images. Using this technology, anyone can take an image and "paint" it in the style embedded in a painting by Vincent Van Gogh or Georgia O'Keefe or Mark Rothko. For *generation/mutation,* the "obvious" next step was to apply the technology to the source image of the project and to generate versions in the style of iconic artists. The result, *generation/mutation v.3.0*, presents a collection of NST generated images.[1]

A closer inspection of the NST images reveals that the current algorithms are a kind of digital "monkey see, monkey do" machines. NST algorithms are incredibly fast but mindless digital robots, powerful digital machines that "learn" by ingesting vast amounts of data and detecting patterns contained in that data, frequently with the aid of processor intensive matrix calculations. NST applications are essentially high capacity mathematical pattern recognition machines, far beyond anything a human brain could perceive and process, and, if trained well, their predictions allow them to simulate patterns based on their analysis of the sampled data. Neural network style transfer algorithms generate simulations based on probabilistic predictions as to what the next pixel in an output image should look like. The predictions are based on patterns detected in the style image and applied to the content image to generate the result image. But no matter how persuasive or convincing NST generated images may be, they are nevertheless only algorithmic simulations of creative behavior, a sophisticated form of digital mimicking.

Intelligent agents simulate intelligent behavior. Creative agents simulate creative behavior. However, we have reached a point where we are no longer able to distinguish human creative actions from the actions of digital simulators—a situation that evokes both amazement and anxiety.

Nearly four hundred years ago, in 1637, the philosopher and mathematician Rene Descartes was the first to see and articulate the need for a method or test to distinguish the actions of human beings from those of sophisticated simulation machines. Descartes thought that even though

> such machines might execute many things with equal or perhaps greater perfection than any of us, they would, without doubt, fail in certain others from which it could be discovered that they did not act from knowledge (Descartes 1637).

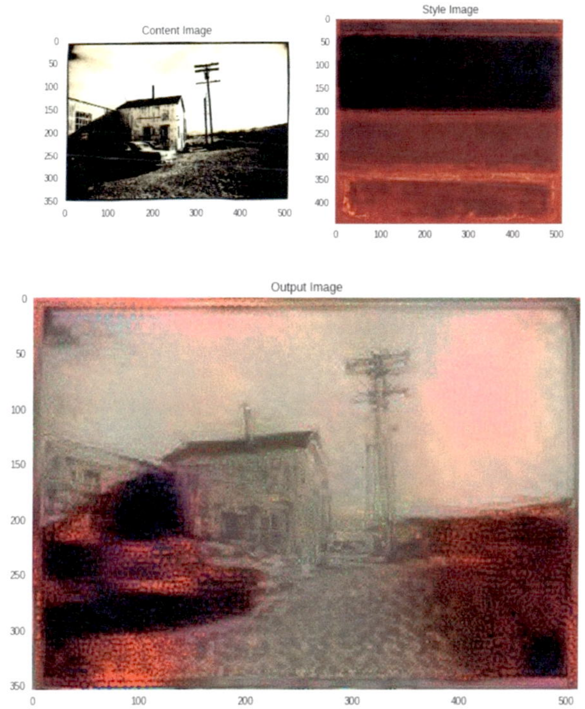

Screenshot 1 – Content, Style, and Output Image for Rothko neural net style transfer

Descartes anticipates that machines will reach a level of technical sophistication where they would perform many tasks significantly better than any human being. But what exactly does he mean by (not) acting from knowledge? And how would we determine that a machine is or is not acting from knowledge?

In his deliberations, Descartes considers two types of *automatons*, ie, mechanical puppets that were a popular form of entertainment in seventeenth century Paris. One of the automatons imitates the looks and behavior of an animal, the other that of a human being. Descartes argues that

> were there such machines exactly resembling organs and outward form an ape or any other irrational animal, we could have no means of knowing that they were in any respect of a different nature from these animals; but if there were machines bearing the image of our bodies, and capable of imitating our actions as far as it is morally possible, there would still remain two most certain tests whereby to know that they were not therefore really men. (Descartes 1637)

In the first test, Descartes aims to show that such machines "could never use words or other signs arranged in such a manner as is competent to us in order to declare our thoughts to others" (Descartes 1637). He admits that it is possible build a machine that produces convincing vocal responses, even short bits of speech, but these bits are not in response to actual conversational inquiries, and the machine will be unable "to reply to what is said in its presence, as men of the lowest grade of intellect can do" (Descartes 1637).[2]

The second test is based on Descartes' belief that automatons, no matter how well built, will have a finite (and relatively small) repertoire of simulations. They are, in a sense, early versions of today's AI expert systems, which easily outperform any human being in some complex skill, but which do not know how to carry on the simplest of conversations about the weather. For Descartes, this is not simply a technical problem like a lack of mechanical skill or engineering abilities. In a much more decisive sense, Descartes' second test is a consequence of his substance dualism in which machines do not and—as a material things made from matter—cannot have reason, which is exclusive to the other of the two fundamental substances: mind.

> It must be morally impossible that there should exist in any machine a diversity of organs sufficient to enable it to act in all the occurrences of life, in the way in which our reason enables us to act (Descartes 1637).

Today, we know that what seemed impossible to Descartes will be part of our own reality very soon. Already, many existing AI systems are sophisticated enough to easily pass either of Descartes' tests. Nevertheless, the AI systems currently in use are indeed "mindless" software programs in Descartes' sense. Generally classified as "weak" AI, they perform specialized human tasks, but without independent intelligence (Wikipedia 2020). In Descartes' terms, these systems lack the ability of conscious, autonomous reasoning; they are unable to employ universal reason in independent (and morally relevant) decision making.

Neural style transfer algorithms are clearly "mindless" software applications in Descartes' sense. Still, they have reached a level where they produce results that are increasingly difficult to distinguished from human actions or products. They are the vanguards of future creative agents, exponentially more powerful expert systems that simulate human creative behavior in ever more startling and amazing ways. NST image generators, on the other hand, will most likely lose their novelty and become just another Photoshop filter, available to millions of users at the click of a mouse.

Today's neural style transfer algorithms are just one of the many developments in AI and machine learning. The current explosion of these technologies marks the dawn of a frightening new age—an age that will change what it means to be human. We are witnessing the dawn of this new age. In its opening fanfare, creative machines and intelligent agents confidently hail the coming disappearance of most human pursuits and professions, including the traditional, human artist.

As disturbing as this disappearance (or radical transformation) of traditional human occupations and pursuits may seem, it also brings new freedoms, radical, previously unimaginable freedoms and new ways of being human that spring from a playful creative intelligence embedded in social connectedness.

The invention of photography in the nineteenth century liberated painting from its bondage to the visible world and the simulation of the appearances of the real. Today's advances in artificial intelligence and machine learning technologies are liberating a new generation of artists from their bondage to traditional art making paradigms.

Human artists will deploy artificial creative agents to produce entirely new genres of artworks—interactive immersions or insertions, hyperreal or augmented interventions—there is no limit to what the deployment of creative agents by human creatives could generate.

The NST images created for the third version of generation/mutation are but a small first step in that direction. In a complete reversal from the google-made images generated by robotic Street View photography, the NST images are *hyperreal* as envisioned by the French philosopher Jean Baudrillard in the nineteen-eighties. For Baudrillard, the hyperreal "is the generation by models of a real without origin or reality." The defining feature of presentations of the hyperreal is that they no longer connected to "a referential being or substance" (Baudrillard 1983).

This absence of the real—and the untethered freedom from any aspects of the real (i.e., physical, objective reality)— elevates the ontological status of the pixel to the ultimate constituent in visualizations of hyper realities. This autonomy of hyperreal imagery prevents any appeal to the real as an objective ground of truth. Hyperreal images are neither true nor false with regards to the actual world; they look like photographic images of something real, but they are not (photomechanical) reproductions of anything real. Reality is no longer needed except perhaps as the original possible world. It is pixels and models alone that generate hyperreal presentations of possible, non-actual worlds. Many popular examples of hyperreal presentations depict persons and situations that look as if they are real but they are not. Because of their "realistic" appearance, hyperreal images and animation tend to create confusion and uncertainty. Not surprisingly, one of the most common uses of hyperreal images can be seen in the spectacular proliferation of deep fake videos and images.

The advances in AI and machine learning and their application in the arts trigger a distinctly modern sense of wonder—a sense of wonder that combines amazement and anxiety in equal measure. For Aristotle, it was a more naïve sense of wonder that brought men to philosophical inquiry. Most important in the current context, Aristotle—like Descartes nearly two thousand years later—also mentions self-moving puppets or marionettes (*ton thaumaton t'automata*), that were so successful in imitating the behavior of animals or people that they evoked astonishment and wonder.[3]

> For all men begin . . . by wondering that things are as they are, as they do about self-moving marionettes, or about the solstices or the incommensurability of the diagonal of a square with the side (*Metaphysics* 983a, Ross translation).

Aristotle mentions automatons as the first of three examples that trigger that deep sense of wonder which is the starting point of philosophical investigations.[4] We have come a long way since the days of Aristotle and the automatons of antiquity, like Archytas' flying bird[5] or the fantastic automatons built by Hephaistos and Daedalus—which to the ancients appeared to feel and think like men.[6] Today's most startling automatons are intelligent and creative agents. An entirely new generation of silicon based automatons, creatures that appear to inhabit a virtually unlimited digital space with seemingly unlimited abilities. Our encounters with them creates perhaps a more anxious sense of wonder, compared to that of the ancients, and is likely to engender an equally new breed of philosophical investigations, prompted by the disappearance of skills and activities that previously were thought to be uniquely human in nature.

The evolution of *generation/mutation* chronicles how machine and AI-driven creative technologies alter the way art and artworks are produced. The role of the artist is caught in a transformative turmoil brought about by the acceleration of technological revolutions and their corresponding social transformations. It is becoming increasingly clear that we are at the threshold of a new age that will question and test what it means to be human. All our traditional human occupations and professions, from truck driver to brain surgeon, from lawyer to artist, are on a path to oblivion. Our traditional ideas about work and value are bound to disintegrate under the weight of AI and machine learning technologies. What remains is the creative spark and ingenuity at the heart of human consciousness, the imagination and energy of creatives and visionaries that have the potential to lead us to new modes of being human.

Notes

[1] The NST images for generation/mutation v.3.0 were generated by an application built on Google's TensorFlow machine learning platform (Google 2019). For more detailed introductions to neural style transfer applications including code samples, see (Yuan 2018), (Ganegedara 2019). A good hands-on neural style transfer tutorial is available at (TensorFlow.Org 2020).

[2] It is an amusing thought experiment to imagine Descartes interacting with any of today's voice controlled devices or reading a summary of his *Meditations* as generated, for example, by GPT-3, the latest iteration of the leading AI text generator (Heine 2020).

[3] Plato, too, used automata in his philosophical discussions. In the Allegory of the Cave, automata play an important part in the creation of the shadow show that the prisoners of the cave mistake for reality.

[4] In traditional readings of the *Metaphysics*, beginning with Thomas Aquinas, greater emphasis is given to eclipses (the movements of the stars and planets) and mathematical paradoxes as triggers of philosophical questioning, since they exhibit greater perfection, leading a more direct way to God as the central object of metaphysical considerations. Taking automata as starting point of inquiries into the nature of "being qua being" shifts the trajectory of the investigations towards an answer to the Delphic admonition "Know thyself!"

[5] Archytas of Terentum (428–347 BC) is credited with building an artificial, self-propelled flying device, a bird-shaped automaton,

most likely propelled by a jet of steam. The device is said to have flown across a distance of 200 yards.

[6] The automatons created by the divine blacksmith Hephaistos and the Athenian craftsman Daedalus were animated metal statues of animals, men, or monsters.

generation/mutation 3.1

AI-sourced neural net style transfer contributions

generated and digitally enhanced by H-Ray Heine

2019

Today abstraction is no longer that of the map, the double, the mirror, or the concept. Simulation is no longer that of a territory, a referential being or substance. It is the generation by models of a real without origin or reality: A hyperreal.

Jean Baudrillard, *Simulacra and Simulation*

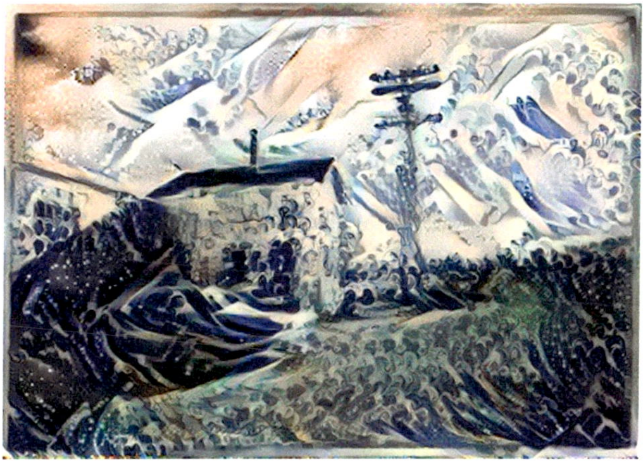

Great Wave NST

DV01 Great Wave NST

Neural style transfer image

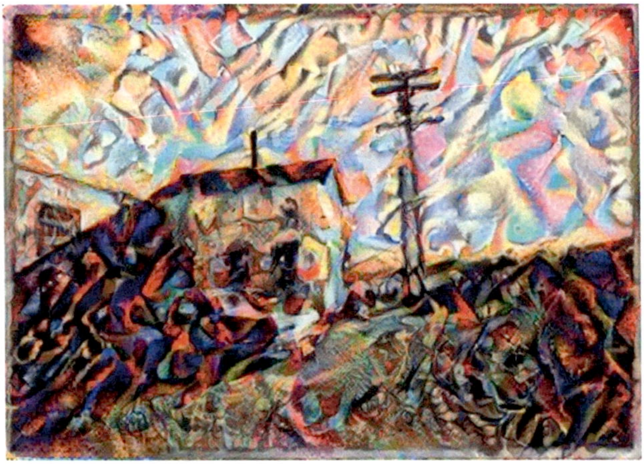

Kandinsky NST

DV01 Kandinsky NST

Neural style transfer image

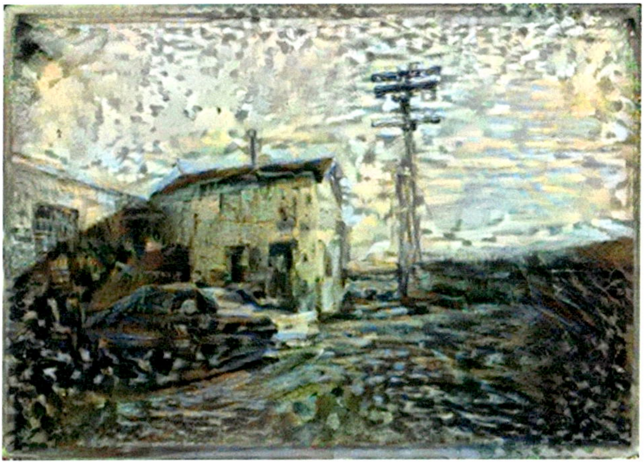

Monet NST

DV01 Monet NST

Neural style transfer image

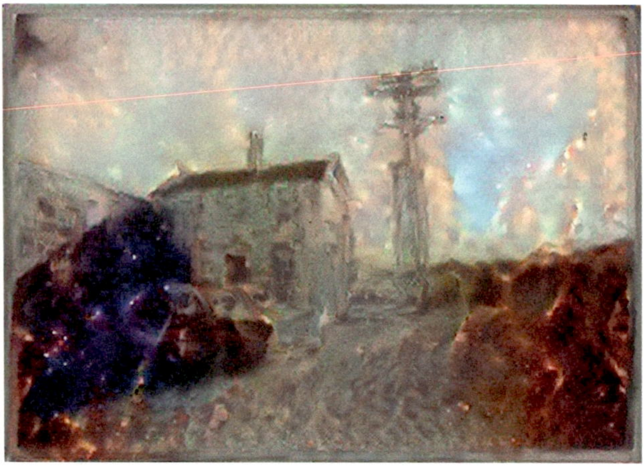

Pillars NST

DV01 Pillars NST

Neural style transfer image

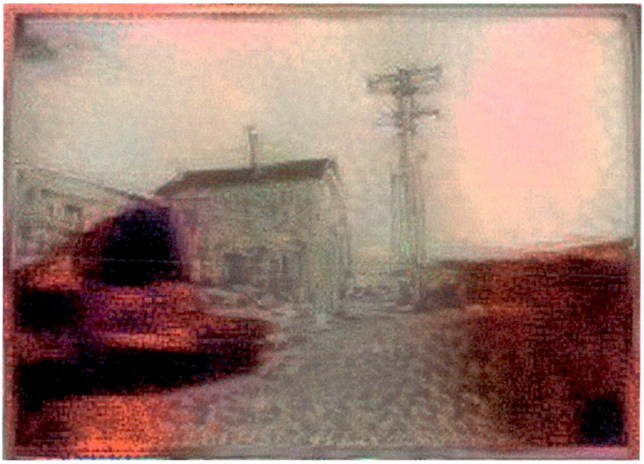

Rothko NST

DV01 Rothko NST

Neural style transfer image

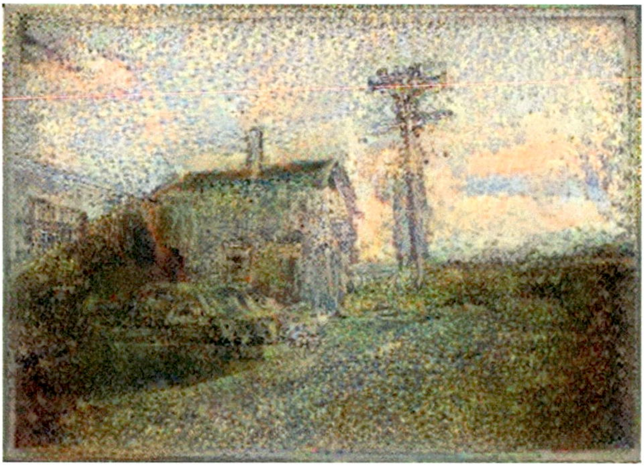

Seurat NST

DV01 Seurat NST

Neural style transfer image

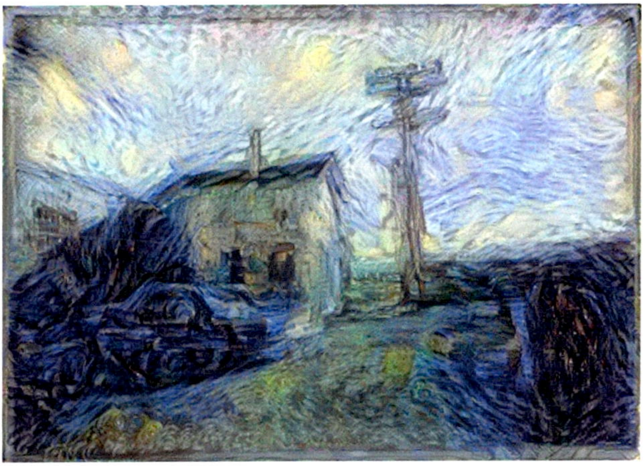

Van Gogh NST

DV01 Van Gogh NST

Neural style transfer image

About the Author

Holger 'H-Ray' Heine is an artist, philosopher, and social impact entrepreneur. He holds a PhD in philosophy from the University of Melbourne, Australia, for his research on Jan Lukasiewicz' early work on Aristotle and the principle of contradiction. He is the author of a translation of Edward Conze's pioneering 1932 work, *The Principle of Contradiction*, (Lexington Books, 2013) and the editor of DIGITALSOULS.COM where he writes occasional posts on new media art, philosophy, and culture.

For more information, please visit: hrayheine.com

Bibliography

Aristotle. 1924. *Metaphysics.* Translated by W.D. Ross. Oxford: Clarendon Press.

Baudrillard, Jean. 1983. *Simulations.* New York, NY: Semiotext(e), Inc.

Brin, Sergey and Lawrence Page. 2016. "The Anatomy of a Search Engine." *Computer Science Department, Stanford University.* 07 12. http://infolab.stanford.edu/~backrub/google.html.

Clade, DC. 2013. *The History of Photoshop as Told by Its Founding Fathers.* April 13. Accessed March 23, 2019. https://petapixel.com/2013/04/13/the-history-of-photoshop-as-told-by-its-founding-fathers/.

Descartes, René. 1637. "A Discourse on Method." *Gutenberg.org.* Edited by John Veitch. Accessed Oct 4, 2020. https://www.gutenberg.org/files/59/59-h/59-h.htm.

Eno, Brian. 2001. "The Big Here and the Long Now." *DIGITALSOULS.COM art | philosophy | media.* Holger 'H-Ray' Heine. May 11. Accessed August 7, 2019. https://digitalsouls.com/the-big-here-and-the-long-now/.

Fontes, Kris. 2012. *Generation Mutation.* Accessed March 16, 2019. https://edex.adobe.com/resource/d9e707ee9f/.

Ganegedara, Thushan. 2019. "Towards Data Science." *Intuitive Guide to Neural Style Transfer.* Jan 8. Accessed Oct 17, 2020. https://towardsdatascience.com/light-on-math-machine-learning-intuitive-guide-to-neural-style-transfer-ef88e46697ee.

Google. 1998. *About Google.* Accessed Sep 01, 2020. https://about.google/.

—. 2019. "An end-to-end open source machine learning platform." *TensorFlow.* Aug 18. Accessed Aug 18, 2019. https://www.tensorflow.org/.

—. 2016. *Company History.* 07 14. https://www.google.com/about/company/history/.

—. 2020. *Explore Street View.* February 8. Accessed February 8, 2020. https://www.google.com/streetview/explore/.

Google Lat Long. 2008. *Street View revisits Manhattan.* May 12. Accessed February 8, 2020. https://maps.googleblog.com/2008/05/street-view-revisits-manhattan.html.

Heine, Holger 'H-Ray'. 2020. *Was this post written by a machine?* Sep 18. Accessed Oct 3, 2020. https://digitalsouls.com/was-this-post-written-by-a-machine/.

Herland, Mamta Baruah. 2004. "Internet & WWW Consequences @ Fine Art." *Mamta Baruah Herland.* Accessed March 16, 2019. http://www.mamtaart.com/publication/Internet-&-WWW-Consequences.pdf.

Independent Curators International. 2020. *do it.* July 13. https://curatorsintl.org/special-projects/do-it.

Internet Live Stats. 2019. *Total Number of Websites.* March 17. http://www.internetlivestats.com/total-number-of-websites/.

Jones, Meghan. 2020. "Here's How Google Street View Gets Its Pictures." *Reader's Digest.* March 22. https://www.rd.com/article/how-google-street-view-gets-its-pictures/.

LeWitt, Sol. 1967. "Paragraphs on Conceptual Art." *Artforum*, June.

Obrist, Hans Ulrich. 2013. *Do It: The Compendium.* Edited by Hans Ulrich Obrist. New York, NY: Independent Curators International/D.A.P.

—. 2014. *Ways of Curating.* New York, NY: Faber and Faber.

Popova, Maria. 2013. *Do It: 20 Years of Famous Artists' Irreverent Instructions for Art Anyone Can Make.* June 03. https://www.brainpickings.org/2013/06/03/do-it-the-compendium-hans-ulrich-obrist/.

Ritchin, Fred. 2013. *What a Photograph Can Accomplish: Bending the Frame.* May 28. Accessed March 23, 2019. http://time.com/3799860/what-a-photograph-can-accomplish-bending-the-frame-by-fred-ritchin/.

Rowland, Allison L., and Chris Ingraham. 2017. *How Google Street View Became An Art Form.* Accessed Sep 01, 2020. https://www.fastcompany.com/40424079/how-google-street-view-spawned-an-accidental-art-form.

Safire, William. 2009. *On Language.* Accessed May 19, 2013. https://www.nytimes.com/2009/02/08/magazine/08wwln-safire-t.html?_r=3&ref=magazine&.

Santos, Miguel. 2019. *Short Biography.* Accessed Mar 16, 2019. http://www.santosmiguel.com/Short_Biography.html.

Shreve, Jenn. 2001. *Anyone for Photoshop Tennis?* September 27. Accessed 2017. https://www.wired.com/2001/09/anyone-for-photoshop-tennis/.

Sontag, Susan. 1977. *On Photography.* New York, NY: Picador.

—. 1977. *On Photography.* New York, NY: Picador.

TensorFlow.Org. 2020. "TensorFlow." *Neural Style Transfer.* 10 30. Accessed 11 13, 2020. https://www.tensorflow.org/tutorials/generative/style_transfer.

Tomkins, Calvin. 1996. *Duchamp: A Biography.* New York, NY: Henry Holt.

W3.ORG. 2019. "The WorldWideWeb browser." *W3.ORG.* December 21. https://www.w3.org/People/Berners-Lee/WorldWideWeb.html.

Whale, George, and Naren Barfield. 2004. *Digital Printmaking (Printmaking Handbooks).* Watson-Guptill Publications.

Wikipedia. 2019. *Adobe Photoshop.* December 28. https://en.wikipedia.org/wiki/Adobe_Photoshop.

—. 2020. *Artificial general intelligence.* Sep 17. Accessed Oct 5, 2020. https://en.wikipedia.org/wiki/Artificial_general_intelligence.

—. 2019. *Crowdsourcing.* March 16. Accessed 2019. https://en.wikipedia.org/w/index.php?title=Crowdsourcing&oldid=887919171.

—. 2018. *Death Valley Junction, California.* September 21. Accessed March 18, 2019. https://en.wikipedia.org/w/index.php?title=Death_Valley_Junction,_California&oldid=860489063.

—. 2020. *Lost Highway (film).* Sep 25. Accessed Sep 26, 2020. https://en.wikipedia.org/wiki/Lost_Highway_(film).

—. 2020. *Marta Becket.* May 4. Accessed Sep 26, 2020. https://en.wikipedia.org/wiki/Marta_Becket.

—. 2016. *Netscape Communicator.* 10 02. https://en.wikipedia.org/wiki/Netscape_Communicator.

—. 2020. *Ready-to-wear.* January 23. https://en.wikipedia.org/wiki/Ready-to-wear.

—. 2018. *Timeline of web search engines.* November 9. Accessed March 17, 2019. https://en.wikipedia.org/w/index.php?title=Timeline_of_web_search_engines&oldid=868049448.

Yuan, Raymond. 2018. "Neural Style Transfer: Creating Art with Deep Learning using tf.keras and eager execution." *Medium.Com.* Aug 3. Accessed Oct 17, 2020. https://medium.com/tensorflow/neural-style-transfer-creating-art-with-deep-learning-using-tf-keras-and-eager-execution-7d541ac31398.

Zhou, XianXia. 2012. *The Future of New Media Art .* Accessed March 16, 2019. https://imagcwp.wordpress.com/2012/05/01/the-future-of-new-media-art-xianxia-zhou-paper-3/.

Artists & Contributors

Jean Beil
Daniel C. Boyer
Ted Bragg
Faith Buck
Tara Camacho
Ian Cartwright
Tom R. Chambers
Keith P. Chevalier
Creepy
Kelly Darke
E_B_A
Corey H. Eiseman
Rob Forsyth
Ron George
Google Street View
Google Earth
Gweedo
Udo Hanten
H-Ray Heine
Jay Heitman
Jaxun
Jon Johnson
Kakupacal
Casey Keeler
Joe Keenan
Scott Lickstein
Oliver Loveday
Mary Lynch
Michael MacKenzie
M. Marshall
Alex McLean
Dmitry Misalin
Carl Patzel
Polina
Martin S. Pribble
Jonathan Prince
Stephanie Rigsby
Miguel Santos
Elisha Sarti
Martin Selman
Emily Smith
Phil Smith
TensorFlow
Donald Trimble
Jeremy Turner
Joe Wakefield
M.G. Wood
Zye Zae

Index

Made in the USA
Las Vegas, NV
03 November 2026

57423532R00098